LITTLE-KNOWN MUSEUMS
IN AND AROUND
BERLIN

LITTLE-KNOWN

MUSEUMS

IN AND AROUND

BERLIN

by Rachel Kaplan

HARRY N. ABRAMS, INC., PUBLISHERS

This book is for Sheila,
whose clear vision and kind heart are a source of guidance and hope.

Editor: Adele Westbrook
Designer: Lorraine Ferguson

Library of Congress Cataloging-in-Publication Data
Kaplan, Rachel.
  Little-known museums in and around Berlin / by Rachel Kaplan.
    p. cm.
  Includes bibliographical references and index.
  ISBN 0–8109–2903–1 (pbk.)
  1. Museums—Germany—Berlin—Guidebooks. 2. Berlin (Germany)—
  Guidebooks. I. Title.
  AM51.B4K36 1999
  069'.0943' 155—dc21   98–30701

Front cover:
The entrance to Kleinglienicke Castle and Park, Berlin.

Back cover:
Marlene Dietrich's clutch bag in a dressing room at the Film Museum, Potsdam.

Rachel Kaplan was educated at the Lycée Français de New York and at Northwestern
University, where she earned a B.S. in Journalism. She is an international correspondent
who has written articles for American, British, French, and Czech publications on a
wide range of subjects. She is the author of two previous books, *Little-Known Museums
In and Around Paris,* and *Little-Known Museums In and Around London,* as well
as the co-author of *A La Découverte des Plus Belles Routes Ile-de-France.* She is also the
president of a cultural tourism company based in Paris, French Links.

Printed and bound in Hong Kong

Harry N. Abrams, Inc.
100 Fifth Avenue
New York, N.Y. 10011
www.abramsbooks.com

CONTENTS

———◆———

Acknowledgments

◆

In an age of cynicism and sensationalism, of pandering and manipulation, it is increasingly rare for a writer to have the opportunity to work with a publisher of outstanding integrity and quality, which succeeds year after year in rising above the all-too-prevalent mass of mediocrity. Moreover, it is even more unusual to find a publisher who is willing to encourage a writer to break new ground and make new discoveries. Such a publisher is Harry N. Abrams, Inc., with the visionary and committed Paul Gottlieb as its president and editorial director, and I have had the great good fortune to be working with him as I developed this series on the Little-Known Museums in major world capitals. I am particularly grateful to him for having given me his whole-hearted endorsement to produce this volume on *Little-Known Museums In and Around Berlin,* at a time when the new capital of Germany is beginning to coalesce. It has turned out to be the most intellectually and emotionally rewarding book that I have ever undertaken—the sort of golden opportunity for which so many writers yearn.

My debt to my brilliant and inspiring editor, Adele Westbrook is equally great. Not only was it her idea to have me research and write this book so that it would be published on the tenth anniversary of the fall of the Berlin Wall, but she has also always shown the utmost faith in me, spurring me to do my best, and convincing me that I was up to the task at hand. Adele is more than a meticulous and caring editor; she also brings tremendous insight to the work in progress, so that the finished book exceeds even my own expectations.

I am equally fortunate to be working with the talented graphic designer, Lorraine Ferguson, on this series; thanks to her, each of the Little-Known Museum books is a visual jewel that people will want to peruse over and over again.

I am also indebted to John Morris, one of the twentieth century's most outstanding photo editors, who helped me to find Sibylle Bergemann, the photographer responsible for the major portions of the illustrations in this book. A member of Germany's Academy of Arts, and one of the founders of Berlin's leading photo agency, Ostkreuz, Sibylle came highly recommended. As a native of East Berlin, Sibylle brought a unique perspective to this project. Born in 1943, one of her first memories is of bombs raining down on a Berlin suburb, destroying her home. When I told her we were going to include a museum about the Stasi in the book, located in the Ministry's former headquarters, she told me how one of the worst days of her life was hearing that her daughter had been held hostage by the Stasi for twenty-four hours for questioning.

Sibylle not only gave her heart and soul to this book—as the beauty and power of her photographs will demonstrate—she taught me many things about Berlin and the German people that I would never have learned otherwise. Through knowing her, I have come to have a greater appreciation for Germany and its complexity. Through working with her, I came to love Germany, far more than I ever anticipated.

From a cultural and historical standpoint I have benefited greatly from the time I was able to spend with the curators and directors of the thirty museums that are featured in this book. Their dedication, their passion, and their scholarship are exemplary, as is their fortitude in the midst of tremendous political flux and government economies. I want to personally thank them all for their invaluable assistance in making *Little-Known Museums In and Around Berlin* a reality: Tommy Spree, Director, Anti-Kriegs Museum; Karl-Heinz Starick, Director, Bauernhaus-u. Gurkenmuseum; Dr. Christian Wolsdorf, Director, Bauhaus Archiv-Berlin Museum für Gestaltung; Dr. Ilse Baer, KPM Archives, (Land Berlin), Belvedere, Museum zur Geschichte des Berliner Porzellans; Prof. Dr. H. Walter Lack, Director of the Museum and Library, Renate Ebbinghaus, Public Relations Director, Botanisches Museum Berlin-Dahlem; Elke Pfeil, Brecht Haus, Brecht-Weigel-Gedenkstätte; Prof. Karl H. Bröhan, Director, Dr. Ingeborg G. Becker, Curator, Bröhan Museum; Dr. Magdalena Moeller, Curator, Brücke Museum-Berlin; Dr. Klaus Goldmann, Director, Museumsdorf Düppel; Guido Altendorf, Director of Exhibitions, Filmmuseum Potsdam; Carolina Winkler, Docent, Gründerzeitmuseum im Gusthaus Mahlsdorf; Dr. Hans-Jürgen Frahm, Castlekeeper, Jagdschloss Grunewald; Erica and Rolf Hoffmann, Gallery Directors, Sabrina van der Ley, Curator, Sammlung Hoffmann; Dr. Ingrid Flindell, Managing Director, Dr. Gudrun Fritsch, Docent, Käthe-Kollwitz Museum; Suzanne Fontaine, Châtelaine, Schloss Kleinglienicke; Dr. Ursel Berger, Curator, Georg-Kolbe Museum; Dr. Barbara Mundt, Director, Kunstgewerbemuseum; Dr. Martin Treu, Director, Lutherhalle Wittenberg; Dr. Barbara Hoffmann, Curator, Dorfmuseum Marzahn, Handwerksmuseum und Friseur museum; Dr. Konstantin Restle, Director, Dr. Martin Elste, Curator, Musikinstrumenten Museum; Steffen Leide, Docent, Forschungs-und Gedenkstätte Normannenstrasse; Dr. Burkardt Güres, Palace Director, Pfaueninsel; Matthias Körner, Director of Public Relations, Fürst Pückler Museum, Park & Schloss Branitz; Dr. Detlef Fuchs, Curator, Dr. Peter Böthig; Curator, Schloss Rheinsberg; Prof. Dr. Winfried Baer, Museums Director, Schloss Charlottenburg, Schinkel Pavilion; Dr. Chana C. Schütz, Curator, Stiftung "Neue Synagogue Berlin-Centrum Judaicum"; Ulrich von Heinz, Director, Schloss Tegel; Florentine C. Bredow, Director, Teddy Museum Berlin; Dr. rer.nat. Klaus Goldmann, Senior Curator, Museum für Vor- und Frühgeschichte; Dr. Bernhard Nick, Director, Zucker Museum. I would also like to thank Dr. Alessandra Galizzi Kroegel for her assistance in Berlin, and for her useful suggestions that facilitated so many of my contacts in the museum community.

On a more personal note, I would like to express my gratitude to Alexandre, who has been an invaluable helpmate and source of encouragement throughout the development and writing of this book. Every writer should be so blessed.

—R.K.

Introduction

◆

In 1972, when the German Democratic Republic was recognized as a sovereign nation-state, it embarked on an ambitious plan to open embassies in the major world capitals. Since the country had little in the way of hard currency to achieve this program, its government came up with the idea of raising six hundred million dollars by selling off fine art from its major museums in Berlin, Dresden, and Leipzig. State museum directors were ordered to set aside pieces that could be sold on the international art market, with the proviso that the quality of each work would be such that "it will make your heart break." Sotheby's was to conduct the auction, and make certain that no representatives of the Federal Republic of Germany would be able to send in a "straw man" to acquire the art.

This plan met with considerable opposition, however. East Germany's state museum directors informed the authorities that it was impossible to make such a selection, and a number of curators and restorers took it upon themselves to sign an open letter protesting such a draconian measure. In an attempt to circumvent this opposition, the Cultural Ministry then issued an order for the directors to compile a list showing the insured prices of the museum's finest works, a request no director could disobey. Based on the prices cited, the plan was for the Ministry to take upon itself the final selection of objects for sale. Fortunately, even after these lists were compiled, the overall operation was cancelled by the East German Communist Party's Central Committee.

"When the authorities failed to collect art from the major state museums in Berlin and Dresden, they took gold medals, coins, and artwork from smaller museums, including city museums," recalls Dr. Klaus Goldmann, senior curator at the Museum of Prehistory and Early History, and one of the co-authors of the book *The Spoils of War.* "Under the code name 'Operation Light,' a department of the Ministry of State Security ordered all agencies in the GDR to look for hidden art treasures, that could be sold, including works to be found in strong rooms and old castles, as well as individual pieces from private collections that had been confiscated when their owners left East Germany. In this they were quite successful, to the extent that it is very hard to trace what they sold. After all, their teacher had been Stalin, who had sold the equivalent of six thousand tons of art in the Thirties through auctions in Berlin, London, and Paris in pursuit of hard currency."

Not only was this account confirmed by other curators with whom I spoke in Berlin, but I was surprised to hear former East Germans tell me that this kind of activity in the former GDR was "normal." As an American who has had the good fortune to grow up in a democracy, I was stunned to learn that a government could treat its national cultural institutions and its citizens with such arrogance and impunity.

Then again, Berlin was like no other European city I have ever known. For fifty years it had been a political pawn in the Cold War, a situation that had culminated in the erection of the Berlin Wall in 1961, the concrete and habitual reminder of the city's political and cultural division. As I tried to imagine living in New York City with a wall dividing the East Side of the city from the West, and to envision that one would have to go to a specific guarded checkpoint in order to visit the Metropolitan Museum, I understood for the first time that this inconceivable situation, had, in fact, been a reality that the German people had endured for years. During my sojourn in Berlin I couldn't help but be mindful of the thousands of Germans who were now able to circulate easily through the city, visiting any museum that caught their fancy—an outing that would have been fraught with almost unimaginable difficulty a decade earlier.

Today's Berlin is a city in flux, and this state of affairs is reflected in its museums. Not only are new museums being erected, but many collections are being reorganized along new lines, and works of art that had been missing since World War II are now finding new, and hopefully, permanent homes. Outside Berlin, Medieval Wittenberg, as well as eighteenth-century Potsdam, Cottbus, Neuruppin, and Rheinsberg are reviving those architectural and cultural heritages that had been neglected in the former East Germany. Nowhere was this brought home to me more vividly than in Rheinsberg, the residence of the Crown Prince Frederick (later known as Frederick the Great), where he had spent some of his happiest and most productive hours writing essays and histories, and composing music. In the Fifties, his castle estate

was converted into East Germany's first sanatorium for diabetics, a decision both practical and political. In the new, idealized Marxist state, the palaces of kings were to be used for rational ends, and were not to remain empty testimonials to an age of despotism. Yet, by the 1980s, even the East German government had begun to realize that it is impossible to create a sound and productive nation if the citizens don't have an authentic and comprehensive notion of their past. The fall of the Wall in 1989 proved resoundingly that one cannot censure or hold back the course of history, just as one cannot profitably erase or deconstruct the past.

Working on the *Little-Known Museums* series, I have discovered that each museum we visit represents not merely a showcase for beautiful or remarkable objects, but a storehouse of history, much of it ignored or forgotten. What is remarkable about the museums in and around Berlin is that many curators are making an attempt to present the past as it was, with its grievously tragic errors, as well as with its artistic achievements.

I know of no other city in the world which has done so much to document the horrors of war and fascism, as well as of terror and totalitarianism in its public cultural institutions. Moreover, I can think of no other metropolis that has done more to show what can happen when ideology, political propaganda, irrational discourse, and blind hate infest art and culture, leading not only to broken, shattered lives, but to unspeakable horror. For those of us who have never experienced the excesses of a totalitarian regime, it is hard to comprehend them. Learning about the cultural and political past of Berlin and its surroundings proved to be not only an enlightening, often exhilarating experience, but a usefully humbling one as well.

One of the unexpected pleasures of working on this book was discovering Germany's extraordinary artistic heritage in architecture, sculpture, painting, goldsmithery, and industrial design. At the same time, I think readers will be as surprised as I was to learn that Berlin had the first anti-war museum, that beet sugar was invented and first developed in Germany, that an ordinary German policeman took it upon himself to save the nation's largest synagogue during the infamous *Kristallnacht*.

It is understandable that the devastation and terror that the Nazis inflicted upon the world continues to haunt people more than half a century later, and has deterred many people from visiting Germany. In the light of my own heritage, I worried about my own possible ambivalence toward this nation's recent past. Much to my surprise and relief, the more I learned about Germany's unusual history and heritage, the more I came to feel a new admiration for the resilience of its people. My greatest hope, in preparing *Little-Known Museums In and Around Berlin* is that it will encourage others, whether ensconced in the comfort of their favorite armchairs or as they walk through the streets of Berlin, to join me in this rediscovery of Germany's complex and intriguing culture.

Hopefully, such excursions will be useful in healing some of the wounds of the past, and in helping to pave the way for a brighter, more life-affirming future.

Numerical Legend for Museum Sites In and Around Berlin

(see Map on pages 14–15)

1 Anti-Kriegs Museum
Anti-War Museum

2 Bauernhaus-u.Gurkenmuseum
The Farmer's House and the Pickle Museum

3 Bauhaus Archiv-Berlin Museum
für Gestaltung
*Bauhaus Archive-Berlin Museum
of Design*

4 Belvedere-Museum zur Geschichte
des Berliner Porzellans
*Belvedere-Museum of the History
of Berlin Porcelain*

5 Botanisches Museum Berlin-Dahlem
Botanical Museum Berlin-Dahlem

6 Brecht Haus-Brecht-Weigel-Gedenkstätte
Brecht House-Brecht-Weigel Memorial

7 Bröhan MuseumBerlin
Bröhan Museum

8 Brücke Museum-Berlin
The Bridge Museum-Berlin

9 Museumsdorf Düppel
Düppel Village Museum

10 Filmmuseum-Potsdam
The Film Museum-Potsdam

11 Gründerzeitmuseum im
Gusthaus Mahlsdorf
*Founders' Museum and Manor
House-Mahlsdorf*

12 Jagdschloss Grunewald
Grunewald Hunting Lodge

13 Sammlung Hoffmann
Hoffmann Collection

14 Käthe Kollwitz Museum
Käthe Kollwitz Museum

15 Schloss Kleinglienicke
Kleinglienicke Castle

16 Georg Kolbe Museum
Georg Kolbe Museum

17 Kunstgewerbemuseum
Museum of Applied Arts

18 Lutherhalle Wittenberg
Luther's Hall Wittenberg

19 Dorfmuseum Marzahn-Sammlungen
Handwerksmuseum und
Friseurmuseum
*Marzahn Village Museum-Collections
from the Handicrafts Museum
and Hairdressing Museum*

20 Musikinstrumenten Museum
Museum of Musical Instruments

21 Forschungs-und Gedenkstätte
Normannenstrasse
*Normannenstrasse Research and
Memorial Center*

22 Pfaueninsel
Peacock Island

23 Fürst Pückler Museum-Schloss
und Park Branitz
*Prince Pückler Museum-Branitz
Castle and Park*

24 Schloss Rheinsberg
Rheinsberg Castle

25 Schinkel Pavillon
Schinkel Pavilion

26 Stiftung "Neue Synagoge Berlin-
Centrum Judaicum"
*The New Synagogue Museum-
The Jewish Center*

27 Schloss Tegel
Tegel Castle

28 Teddy Museum Berlin
The Berlin Teddy Museum

29 Museum für Vor- und Frühgeschichte
Museum of Prehistory and Early History

30 Zucker Museum
Sugar Museum

Map of Museum Sites In and Around Berlin

(see Numerical Legend on pages 12–13)

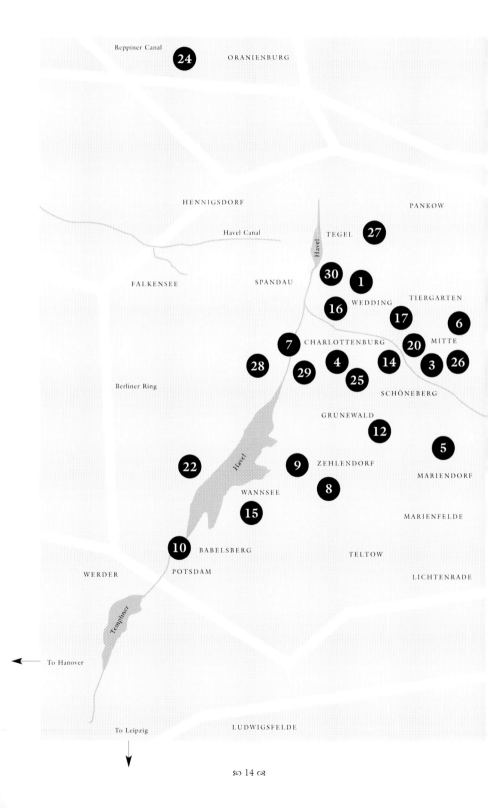

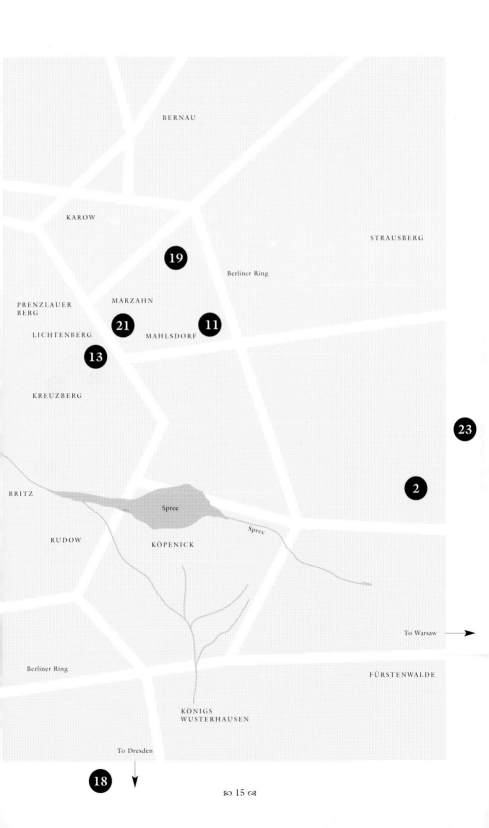

Anti-Kriegs Museum

Anti-War Museum

21 Brüsseler Strasse
Berlin 13353
Tel: 454–90110

Open every day
4:00 P.M. to 8:00 P.M.

U-Bahn: 9 to Amrumer Strasse

THE STOREFRONT ANTI-WAR MUSEUM
IN THE WORKING-CLASS
DISTRICT OF WEDDING
OPENED ON JANUARY 30, 1998,
SIXTY-FIVE YEARS TO THE DAY THAT
ADOLF HITLER BECAME
CHANCELLOR OF GERMANY.

F O R Berliners who lived through World War II, this bunker brings back many memories: the warning sound of the sirens signaling an air raid, the blast of rockets, the awful amalgam of resignation and terror, of wondering whether one's home would still be standing when the bombing had stopped and everyone could emerge from the cellar's depths. It's all there: the inflatable bed for children, which had to be periodically pumped up with fresh air, the suitcases packed with important papers and prized possessions, the small closet filled with medicine and bandages, the signs that warned against talking so the shelter wouldn't run out of oxygen and people wouldn't suffocate, as well as the old *Volksempfämger* radio that Hitler and Goebbels had wanted installed in every German home.

This bunker is a highlight in the tour of Berlin's Anti-War Museum, which, in its latest incarnation, is located in a four-room storefront space in the working-class district of Wedding. "Those who build bunkers, wage wars," notes the museum's director, Thomas Spree. "Hitler began building his bunkers very early. What's notable about our bunker is the door—it has over 400 inscriptions on it, indicating the date, time, and air-raid warning given since the start of the war. We want to make sure such bunkers are never built again in Germany."

Instead of extolling celebrated generals and battles, the aim of this museum (which is supported and funded by the German Government), is to document and discourage an insidious and perverse militarism

who had marched off to war singing and cheering, soon discovered the deadly reality of trench warfare. In a letter dated October 27, 1918, a young student wrote shortly before being killed: "This is not an honest war. The men in the Fatherland who want to continue the war know how it looks here and what's really going on. If people knew the condition our soldiers are in, they wouldn't be able to go on like this . . . "

There are no words that can adequately describe the series of photographs by a Berlin surgeon of soldiers who had been mutilated and disfigured by mines and schrapnel. Some of the wounded had to undergo as many as forty operations to have their faces reconstructed to some semblance of normalcy. Such ghastly portraits are exceedingly rare, since many wounded veterans refused to be photographed, fearing their families and friends would never wish to see them again.

which has been responsible for so much of this century's carnage and tragedy. While the museum has set aside space for temporary exhibitions on current global conflicts, its particular focus remains the rise of German militarism and its disastrous consequences, particularly during World War I and World War II.

Antique painted lead soldiers that young boys loved to line up into battle formations, old-fashioned paper-doll gunners and saber-brandishing cavaliers, decks of cards decorated with the German Panzer tank, and the "Game of Besieging," a popular war game manufactured before World War I, as well as storybooks glorifying soldiers' heroism, illustrate how bellicose tendencies are fostered in children from an early age.

Less than a decade after playing these seemingly innocent games, thousands of young German soldiers,

THIS WORLD WAR I "PICKLE" HELMET
FAILED TO SHIELD MANY SOLDIERS
FROM THE DIRE CONSEQUENCES OF WAR.

KÄTHE KOLLWITZ'S RENOWNED POSTER,
NEVER AGAIN WAR,
DOMINATES A ROOM FULL OF
EXHIBITS SHOWING
THE INSTRUMENTS AND RESULTS OF WARFARE.

It was easier to palliate the horrors of World War I with death certificates stamped with an Iron Cross and signed by Kaiser Wilhelm II, which carried this citation from the Bible's Book of John: "We shall give our lives for our brothers." German parents proudly displayed paintings or photographs of their sons in full military regalia, or elaborately framed photographs of a fallen loved one with messages such as this one: "You have died too young. We'll miss you very much. You have been so good and loving; we will never forget you."

Far away from the front, it was common for families to collect home furnishings and accessories decorated with military symbols and figures. A decorative cannon with lead balls, a butter mold in the shape of an iron cross, a china fruit dish decorated with the printed image of Field Marshall Von Hindenberg, a patriotic sampler embroidered with the phrase *Deutschland über Alles (Germany Over All)*, and a letter opener made from a souvenir hand-grenade removed from a soldier's leg, reveal to what extent certain German households revered the military mystique.

The exhibits of masks against biological and chemical warfare, as well as photographs of modern German military equipment being used by other nations, underscores the point that even after a century of unspeakable carnage, the global armaments industry has continued to flourish. "Every sixty seconds, 1.5 million dollars are spent on the production of weapons," maintains Spree.

Undaunted by the challenges of

opposing a lucrative industry, Spree is pleased that many German teachers make a point of visiting this museum with their classes. "The school children are often very moved by what they see," he notes. "The questions they ask most frequently are 'How do wars begin?' and 'What would be the best way to preserve the peace?' "

Yet, few visitors who come to this museum, know that Spree's grandfather, Ernst Friedrichs (1894–1967), founded the world's first Anti-War Museum in 1925 in Berlin. In an engrossing documentary made in 1989, visitors learn how Friedrichs, the thirteenth child born to a washerwoman and a bank assistant in Breslau, Silesia (now part of Poland), felt compelled to dedicate most of his life to the cause of peace. Arriving in Berlin prior to World War I, Friedrichs (who had studied acting in Breslau), became an actor in the Imperial Theater at Potsdam, where he appeared until 1917. Having been sent to entertain the troops at the front, he was shocked to discover that Kaiser Wilhelm's promise "I lead you to glorious times," was a sham.

Refusing to enlist in the German army, he was first sent to prison, then committed to an insane asylum where he remained until the end of the war. Although politically active in the left-wing Spartacists group, Friedrichs' main avocation was developing a forum for disseminating his pacifist ideas. In 1925, with the support of the Quakers and other peace groups, he opened the Anti-War Museum at 29 Parochialstrasse, on the ground floor of a picturesque seventeenth-century building. Over the entrance, an insignia depicting two arms holding a broken rifle, was to become an emblem adopted by pacifist organizations around the world. "It was most likely the first museum dedicated to peaceful political solutions," notes Spree. (The building housing the museum was destroyed during World War II.) Käthe Kollwitz, Heinrich Zille (best remembered for his portrayals of working-class Berlin), Otto Dix, and George Grosz all showed their work in this museum. The most famous lithographed poster by Käthe Kollwitz from this period carries the slogan *Nie wieder Krieg! (Never Again War!)* and depicts a young man with upraised arms and two fingers extended taking the solemn oath to the German state.

Friedrichs' left-wing sympathies and pacifist views did not find favor with the Nazis, who desecrated the Anti-War Museum in March 1933. Shortly afterward, the SA converted the museum into a locale for their meetings, where opponents of the Nazi regime were tortured. Friedrichs' anti-war and pro-Communist activities caused him to be convicted thirteen times between 1923 and 1933, before he and his family were forced to flee to Belgium by way of Czechoslovakia and Switzerland. Able to save the most important exhibits and publications from destruction,

"Hurra-Tüte"
Wehrmachtshelm deutscher Soldaten im
II. Weltkrieg

Grabentaschenlampe

Friedrichs opened his second Anti-War Museum in Brussels in 1936. Four years later, when the German army invaded Belgium, the museum was ransacked and forced to close.

Although Friedrichs was arrested and sent to an internment camp in Gurs, France, he was able to flee and join the French Resistance, where he remained until the Liberation. After the war, he returned to Berlin and was awarded a government pension, which compensated for some of the suffering he and his family had endured during the Nazi regime. Alarmed by Germany's rearmament during the Cold War, in 1950 he asked Berlin's Mayor Ernst Reuter to let him transform the city's most famous landmark showing the futility of war—the 207-foot-high ruined tower of the Kaiser Wilhelm Memorial Church on the Breitscheidplatz—into another Anti-War Museum. When his request was refused, Friedrichs died a broken-hearted man.

Fifteen years after his grandfather's death, inspired by Friedrichs' work, and the growing peace movement in Germany, Spree opened Berlin's third Anti-War Museum in 1982, relocating it twice before installing it at 21 Brüsseler Strasse. While few pieces remain from Friedrichs' original collection, the irrepressible spirit of this courageous pacifist remains omnipresent. "Berlin, which was destroyed by Nazi megalomania, should be a center for making peace," says Spree, his voice filled with quiet passion and determination. Hopefully, this progressive and thought-provoking museum will be instrumental in fulfilling this vital and humane objective.

THIS TWO-HUNDRED-YEAR-OLD WOODEN FARMHOUSE,
WITH ITS THATCHED-AND-TILED ROOF,
ONCE SHELTERED THE FAMILY, AS WELL AS A COW AND A PIG.

Bauernhaus-u. Gurkenmuseum

The Farmer's House and the Pickle Museum

An der Dolzke 6
03222 Lübbenau-Lehde
Tel: 03542–89990

Open every day
10:00 A.M. to 6:00 P.M.
March 1 to October 31.
Otherwise, call ahead to make
special arrangements for a visit out
of season. (Note: When the ice
freezes over on the Spree, both the
farmer's house and pickle museum
are opened to the public.)
Group tours of six or more can
be arranged in advance throughout
the year.

By train: A one-hour trip from
Berlin's Lichtenburg station
to Lübbenau, followed by a ten-
minute shuttle-service from the
station. (During the winter
months, only taxi service is
available.)

By car: Take the Autobahn A-13
to Lübbenau, then follow the signs
to Lehde. A billboard will indicate
the direction to the nearby
Bauernhaus-u. Gurkenmuseum.

Four restaurants on the premises,
as well as boating, hotel, and
guest house facilities.

NINETY minutes southeast of
Berlin lies the heart of the
Oberspreewald, 500-square-kilo-
meters of woodland overrun by 300
channels fed from the Spree River
and crisscrossed with man-made
canals, a region that the German
writer Theodor Fontane compared to
"Venice as it might have been 1,500
years ago." It is here in the village of
Lehde that one can find a charming
homage to a rural way of life that
all but disappeared with farm collec-
tivization in the former German
Democratic Republic. Until 1931, the
town could only be reached by punt
or by crossing the frozen channels on
skates. Farm animals and harvested
crops were transported by boat from
the fields to market.

In summer, this verdant and unsul-
lied landscape is a mecca for nature-
lovers who enjoy the company of
storks, beavers, badgers, otters, deer,
and foxes in their natural setting—
a rich and varied biosphere that has
been placed under UNESCO's
protection since 1991. Much of the
local population descends from the
Slavic Sorbs who settled in both
Saxony and Brandenburg in the
Middle Ages. As many as 100,000
Sorbs (whose language resembles
both Czech and Slovak), still live in
the region, retaining their traditional
costumes and festivals, which add an
unexpected vibrancy and animation
to the untamed terrain.

Visitors to Lehde are surprised to
find the only extant farmhouse built
over 250 years ago in the Spreewald,
the Bauernhaus, whose striking façade
of dark-stained oak and sloping roof
made of tightly woven reeds and slate

THIS STORAGE SHED CONTAINS A NUMBER OF INDISPENSABLE HOUSEHOLD TOOLS,
SUCH AS A BUTTER CHURN AND A REED CUTTER.
(THE REEDS THAT GREW ALONG THE BANKS OF THE RIVER SPREE
WERE USED FOR MAKING BASKETS AND RUSH SEATS.)

tiles reflects the traditional building materials once common to this region. Restored in 1995 with the intent of retaining the utmost in authenticity, the house demonstrates the rigors of farm life in the Spreewald. Until the middle of this century, most of its inhabitants subsisted from fishing and hunting, and from the cultivation of market gardens, which yielded onions, potatoes, cabbage, cucumbers, and horseradish.

This farm (like the others in the region), had to depend on fresh water being brought by cart and later by truck twice a week, since it had no running water. Water for washing and cleaning was drawn from the stream in front of the house. Animals and people lived side by side in the Bauernhaus, the kitchen opening onto the barn, where the pigs were kept. Outside the barn hang the nets used for catching fish in the Spree, and the rack where slaughtered pigs

THIS BEDROOM SHOWS THE SORBS' LOVE OF
BRIGHTLY COLORED FABRICS AND STENCILED FURNITURE.
SUCH COSTUMES ARE STILL WORN TODAY BY THE SLAVIC SORBS
ON TRADITIONAL FEAST DAYS.

were once bled before being prepared for the family's consumption. Next to it is a meticulously crafted wood-and-reed dog house where the farm's dog once slept.

According to the museum's director, Karl-Heinz Starick, four generations of the Mühlan family lived in this house until 1909, earning their livelihood by growing onions and potatoes. Most of the objects in the house, including the well-thumbed Bible and the faded pho-tographs, clothes, and headgear, once belonged to this family. As many as a dozen people shared living quarters in this cramped, four-room, two-story house, which consists of a kitchen, a combination living room and bedroom, an upstairs sewing room, a storage room, and a spare bedroom.

"When a couple got married they were permitted to sleep in the upstairs bedroom for three weeks, so they could have some privacy," notes Starick. "Then they had to return to

the downstairs bedroom. At other times, the bedroom was used by the great-grandparents if they were still living."

To help visitors appreciate the way farmers worked and lived, the museum goes to great lengths to present a wide array of machinery, tools, and utensils that were used on the farm: cream separators, butter churns, flax-and-linen spinning wheels, even a hand-cranked linen press. Seeing the fully-furnished

kitchen, its walls gaily decorated with floral potato stencils, it is not so difficult to envision the farmer's wife preparing a hearty fish soup on the old kindling-fed cast-iron stove. A hand-painted cupboard, a sideboard filled with ceramic dishes in a wide array of floral patterns, as well as a broad assortment of crockery, baskets, and spoons, enhance the room's rusticity.

The house's downstairs sleeping and living quarters are dwarfed by the

WHEN THE SPREEWALD ICES OVER IN WINTER
IT IS OPEN SEASON FOR
BOTH SKATERS AND CYCLISTS.

broad oak canopy bed where three
generations of Sorbs once slept.
Those family members who didn't
have a bed were forced to make do
with a straw pallet, which they made
up every night. Next to the bed
are freestanding cupboards where the
family's clothes were kept. Despite
these spartan living conditions, every
attempt was made to keep the home
clean and attractive—the walls are
decorated with religious pictures
and faded family photographs, the
windows hung with lace and linen
curtains. The family's clothes were
made in the upstairs sewing room;
different colored embroidered
lace-trimmed fichus and white cotton
eyelit aprons (no two of which are
alike) show the traditional finery
women once wore to church and on
local feast days.

Next to the Bauernhaus is the
Gurkenmuseum, a former pickle manufactory that has been converted into
an exhibition space demonstrating

THESE HANDMADE BARRELS COULD HOLD
AS MANY AS THREE HUNDRED CUCUMBERS
PICKLED IN BRINE,
OR UP TO THREE-AND-A-HALF TONS OF SAUERKRAUT.

how pickles were once made in the Spreewald. Prior to industrialized food processing, cucumbers that were harvested in this region were brought by boat down the channels of the Spree, and then by horse-drawn cart to a central loading point where they were sorted before being put into barrels of salted and flavored brine. As many as 300 cucumbers were stored and pickled in a single barrel. Other farmers also made sauerkraut, and it was not uncommon for up to three-and-a-half tons of this salted cabbage to be stored in enormous barrels, examples of which can be found in the Gurkenmuseum.

Black-and-white period photos, as well as a specially-made video in German and English, show that cucumber pickling was a strenuous, labor-intensive process that involved all farmers on the Spreewald earlier in this century. A highlight for visitors is being able to sample the variety of homemade pickles: sweet, sour, mustard, garlic, and herb. With such variety, it's not surprising that Fontane called this region "the Fatherland of the sour pickle."

Thanks to the fine restoration of the Bauernhaus and the lively Gurkenmuseum, visitors from all over the world can now discover the rich heritage of the Oberspreewald, an area in Germany that is exceptional in both natural beauty and in rural traditions.

The Bauhaus Archive-Berlin Museum of Design

Klingelhöferstrasse 14
10785 Berlin
Tel: 254–00–20

**Open Wednesday through Monday
10:00 A.M. to 5:00 P.M.**

U-Bahn: 1 or 4 to Nollendorfplatz
Bus: 100, 129, 187, 341 X9

ADJUSTABLE metal reading lamps, tubular-steel dining chairs, striking sans-serif, lower-case typefaces, concrete prefabricated housing, abstract painting and kinetic sculpture—all things which have become commonplace in the twentieth century—owe their existence at least in part, to a school of art and design founded in Weimar, Germany, in 1919 and closed by the Nazis in 1933. During its brief existence, this school also spurred a revolution in art education with its *Vorkurs* ("Basic Course"), which offered a serious investigation of materials, color theory, and three-

THE BAUHAUS ARCHIVE AND BERLIN MUSEUM FOR DESIGN
WAS BUILT BETWEEN 1976 AND 1978
AND WAS BASED ON PLANS MADE BY THE SCHOOL'S FOUNDER, WALTER GROPIUS.
(GROPIUS, WHO WAS BORN IN BERLIN IN 1883,
NEVER LIVED TO SEE THE BUILDING COMPLETED.)

THIS RARE ABSTRACT STONE SCULPTURE BY OTTO WERNER,
MADE IN THE BAUHAUS SCULPTURE WORKSHOP,
SETS OFF A SHOWCASE FILLED WITH EXAMPLES OF
THE SCHOOL'S INDUSTRIAL DESIGNS.

dimensional design—a program that continues to be used in many art and design schools to this day.

This school was the Bauhaus (literally the Building House), which succeeded in achieving three fundamental objectives that revolutionized twentieth-century design, outlined in a manifesto by its founder and director, the acclaimed architect Walter Gropius (1883–1969). Its first goal was to rescue all the arts from isolation and to train future craftsmen, painters, and sculptors to embark upon cooperative projects that would integrate all their skills. The second was to elevate the status of crafts to that of the fine arts. "The artist is an exalted craftsman," Gropius's Bauhaus manifesto proclaimed. "Let us then create a new guild of craftsmen without the class distinctions that raise an arrogant barrier between craftsman and artist!"

Its third endeavor was to free itself from the dependence of public subsidy by selling its products and designs to the public and to industry.

A tour of the spacious and airy Bauhaus Archives and Museum of Design erected between 1976 and 1978 on the Tiergarten side of Berlin's Landwehrkanal (a late work of Walter Gropius, who did not live to see its completion), documents the achievements of this unique institution and presents a comprehensive overview of the school's experimental designs and artwork from such distinguished talents as Wassily Kandinsky, Paul Klee, Lyonel Feininger, Laszlo Moholy-Nagy, Oskar Schlemmer, Josef Albers, Marcel Breuer, and Ludwig Mies van der Rohe.

In this age of specialization, it is heartening to learn to what extent the Bauhaus created an environment in which iconoclastic geniuses could blossom in a multiplicity of fields. One need look no further than Laszlo Moholy-Nagy, the Hungarian painter and teacher on the staff of the Bauhaus at Weimar and Dessau from 1923 to 1928. Indebted to Russian Constructivism, as well as to an intensive study of kinetics, in 1929 he created the *Lichtrequisit* (Light Space Modulator), the first large, three-dimensional kinetic sculpture in the history of art, whose metal and clear plastic structure was made to rotate slowly through the use of an electric motor. He was also the first artist to maintain that a work of art was reproducible—a concept he demonstrated with his "telephone pictures," executed by another hand according to precise instructions given over the phone.

This indefatigable talent also became keenly involved in practical, everyday design, inspiring the Bauhaus metal workshop to switch from a craft-oriented silversmith's shop to one that produced prototypes of everyday objects which could be mass-produced, such as jugs, tea and coffee sets, lamps, and industrial lighting. Persuading students that steel plate, and not silver, would satisfy the most pressing needs of design, he inspired the creation of what have now become classic metal swivel bedside and table lamps, as well as versions made of glass and polished steel, by such outstanding designers as Marianne Brandt, Wilhelm Wagenfeld, Christian Dell, and Hin Brendendieck, examples of which are showcased in the museum.

A striking display of wood and tubular metal chairs demonstrates how the school's carpentry workshop was the most successful in developing models for industry, many of which are still being fabricated. The designer Marcel Breuer made the first arm-chairs with nickel-plated tubular steel (a choice inspired by his bicycle's tubular chrome handlebars), and fitted them with leather or cloth backs, seats, and arm rests. His pioneering use of this industrial material would later inspire other designers, including Mies van der Rohe, whose quilted handmade leather and chrome Barcelona chair (also on display) is still being produced today.

The school not only set trends in painting, sculpture, and home furnishings design, but in lettering and advertising, as well. Herbert Bayer, who ran the typography work-shop, not only designed a new bold and simple typeface, but changed the spelling of German words, doing away with the capitalization of nouns and subjects in sentences. He argued that lower-case alone was more economical because it required one alphabet instead of two, and would give perfectly legible texts once readers got used to it.

Although the Bauhaus succeeded in making many industrial contacts during its early years in Weimar, it also antagonized local craftsmen who felt their livelihood was being threat-ened. When a right-wing government took control of Thuringia in 1924, the school's funding was cut and it was forced to seek a new home in Dessau, in the tiny state of Anhalt. Gropius designed innovative flat-roofed, streamlined, functional, and assertively modern premises for the school, which included teaching and workshop areas, a theater, a canteen, a gymnasium, and twenty-eight studio flats for students above which was a roof garden. During this period the architecture and interior design department collaborated on an exper-imental low-cost housing develop-ment at Dessau-Törten, built with standardized components (concrete, steel, and glass), which were manufac-tured at the site. These methods demonstrated that standardization made for speed and economy, while on-site manufacturing reduced transportation costs.

In 1928, Gropius resigned his directorship to return to private practice and nominated the Swiss architect Hannes Meyer as his successor. Meyer, a Left-wing intellectual, who believed that the architect's role was mainly utilitarian and should aim to improve the lifestyle of the common man, used the Bauhaus architecture and interior design departments to plan and build the innovative German Trade Union School in Bernau, a model of which is displayed in the museum. While he lent substance to the school's architecture and planning courses by conducting ground-breaking sociological and biological studies (which were hardly standard practice at the time), his anti-aesthetic approach to architecture was opposed by many students and faculty members.

In 1930, Meyer was ousted in a staff coup, with the backing of Dessau's city council, and replaced by Ludwig Mies van der Rohe, an architect whose main commissions came from wealthy private clients. While Mies van der Rohe attempted to reorganize the school along traditional lines, eventually transforming the Bauhaus into an academy of architecture, the school nonetheless encountered virulent opposition from the Nazi Party. Attacked for being too cosmopolitan and therefore anti-German, the Bauhaus was equated with modernism, Bolshevism, and Jewishness. The Jewish nature of the Bauhaus was attributed to the school's preference for flat-roofed architecture, which the Nazis maintained came from subtropical regions and reflected a Jewish legacy.

THESE PHOTOGRAPHS OF BAUHAUS STUDENT ANTICS AT DESSAU
CONTRAST SHARPLY WITH THE SEVERE CHAIRS,
WHICH WERE DESIGNED BY MARCEL BREUER, ERICH DIECKMANN,
HIN BREDENDIECK, AND VERA MIYER-WALDECK.

THESE GLASS DISPLAY CASES PRESENT SOME OF THE BAUHAUS STUDENTS' EARLY WORK
FROM THE POTTERY, SILVERSMITH, AND METAL WORKSHOPS,
DEMONSTRATING THE SCHOOL'S EVOLUTION FROM HANDMADE DESIGNS,
SUCH AS THE CERAMIC JUG IN THE FOREGROUND,
TO THE INDUSTRIAL TABLE LAMP WITH ITS GLASS STEM AND BASE AND FROSTED GLOBE
(1923–24) BY WILHELM WAGENFELD AND KARL J. JUCKER.

Shortly after the Nazis gained control of Dessau's city council in 1932, the parliament seized the opportunity to rescind the school's grant and terminate all staff contracts. Nazi stormtroopers then occupied the school, breaking windows, and throwing files, tools, and other equipment into the street below. Only a vociferous international campaign stopped them from razing the site altogether.

In a last attempt to rescue the Bauhaus, Mies van der Rohe tried to re-establish the school as an entirely private institution in a defunct telephone factory in the Steglitz suburb of Berlin. Hitler's appointment to the office of Federal Chancellor in January 1933, however, sealed the school's fate. A student at the Berlin Bauhaus, Pius Pahl, recalls the school's final hours. "The end came on April 11, 1933, during the first days of summer term. Early in the morning police arrived with trucks and closed the Bauhaus. Bauhaus members without proper identification (and who had this?) were loaded on the trucks and taken away." On August 10, 1933, Mies van der Rohe notified the remaining students that the faculty had voted to dissolve the Bauhaus, citing "the difficult economic situation of the institute." It was only a matter of time before most of the faculty at the Bauhaus would undergo a period of personal persecution (at least twelve members died in concentration camps), or be forced to emigrate.

Considering its modest number of students (1,250 in total), its limited funding, and the fact that its history

coincided with the turbulent and shaky Weimar Republic and the rise of Nazi Germany, it is all the more remarkable that the Bauhaus is still regarded by many individuals as one of the most significant artistic movements of the century. Even though some critics and designers now question the lack of individuality and whimsy in its designs, few dispute the major impact the Bauhaus has had on everything from architecture to mass-produced household objects.

"The Bauhaus remains important because it bridged the gap between science and art, craft and industry," notes Dr. Christian Wolsdorff, the museum's curator. "While we cannot replicate the Bauhaus today, designers still receive inspiration from this museum." The questions the Bauhaus raised about the nature of good design, are still being asked, making this valuable institution a source of ideas which still can be explored profitably today.

BETWEEN 1830 AND 1840, THE ROYAL MANUFACTORY OF PORCELAIN
PRODUCED VASES DEPICTING SITES SUCH AS
THE SCHLOSS CHARLOTTENBURG (LEFT),
AND THE SCHLOSSKAPELLE AT STOLZENFELS ON THE RHINE (RIGHT).
(PHOTO: STIFTUNG PREUSSISCHE SCHLÖSSER UND GÄRTEN BERLIN-BRANDENBURG,
SCHLOSS CHARLOTTENBURG, FOTOTHEK)

Belvedere-Museum zur Geschichte des Berliner Porzellans

Belvedere-Museum of the History of Berlin Porcelain

Charlottenburg Palace Park
Charlottenburg-Berlin
Tel: 32091–212

Open Tuesday through Sunday
10:00 A.M. to Noon and
1:00 P.M. to 5:00 P.M.
April 1 to October 31.
Closed Monday and holidays.

U-Bahn: 7 to Richard Wagner Platz
Bus: 109, 110, 145, X21, X26

In 1788, Friedrich Wilhelm II, Frederick the Great's nephew, weary of the tedious ceremonies at court, commissioned Carl Gotthard Langhans (the architect of Berlin's Brandenburg Gate), to design a charming three-story tea pavilion on the palace grounds at Charlottenburg. With its oval floor plan, domed roof, and curved projecting bays, the almond-green and white structure is a charming example of early Neoclassical architecture enlivened by touches of the Baroque. Known

CARL GOTTHARD LANGHANS, THE ARCHITECT OF BERLIN'S BRANDENBURG GATE,
DESIGNED THIS TEA PAVILION ON THE GROUNDS OF THE CHARLOTTENBURG PALACE.
THE EARLY NEOCLASSICAL BUILDING, KNOWN AS THE BELVEDERE,
HOUSES THE MUSEUM DEVOTED TO
THE HISTORY OF THE ROYAL MANUFACTORY OF PORCELAIN (KPM).

THIS WHITE BISCUIT PORCELAIN BUST
OF FREDERICK THE GREAT
BY F. E. MEYER (1778),
SUGGESTS THE ALOOFNESS AND
THE SARCASTIC BENT OF THE MAN
WHO FOUNDED THE ROYAL
MANUFACTORY OF PORCELAIN (KPM).

henceforth as the Belvedere (meaning "beautiful view"), the teahouse overlooks a stunning panorama of the grounds and palace at Charlottenburg. Its location along the Spree proved ideal for Friedrich Wilhelm's mistress, the cultivated Countess Lichtenau, who would cross the river by boat to meet her lover for intimate evenings of chamber music, dancing, and séances of Rosicrucianism.

It's a pity that visitors can no longer see the magnificent gilded boiseries and fruitwood parquet flooring that once graced this jewel-like structure, as these were utterly destroyed by bombs during World War II, along with most of the furnishings. Nonetheless, like a phoenix risen from the ashes, the Belvedere has not only been restored to its former glory, but contains an incomparable treasure—reputedly the world's finest collection of eighteenth- and early-nineteenth-century Berlin porcelain, most of it from the Royal Manufactory of Porcelain (KPM) founded by Frederick the Great.

A tour of this enchanting museum (which begins from the top floor downward), offers visitors a fascinating overview of Berlin porcelain from its very beginnings, revealing its technical and aesthetic evolution. Both connoisseurs and amateurs are bound to be impressed by the Rococo period's hand-painted Watteau- and Boucher-inspired motifs and finely gilded dinnerware, as well as by the consummate skill and artistry of Neoclassical porcelain, which replicates with great exactitude minute mosaics and such semi-precious stones as lapis lazuli and porphyry.

Seeing such exceptional pieces, one is not surprised to learn that when Napoleon conquered Berlin in 1806, he not only emptied KPM's treasury, but encouraged the Empress Josephine to commission a number of porcelain services for the French imperial dinner table (none of which were ever paid for).

This novel museum also enhances our understanding of the popularity of certain types of porcelain services no longer manufactured today. One example is the delicate yet sturdy *trembleuse:* a saucer with a high, reticulated tray securing the cup, intended to prevent spillage on costly silk dresses, a serious risk during an outdoor picnic. Two elaborately gilded rose-topped porcelain cloches— among the rarest items on display— once protected food from any loose powder and hair that might fall from a footman's wig. The stems of crystal goblets used to fit neatly into the scalloped rim of an ice-filled porcelain bowl, making it possible to chill glasses before they were filled with wine. The *solitaires* and *déjeuners,* (used for breakfast only) are still carefully packed inside their satin-lined, morocco-leather trunks—a necessary precaution for solo travelers who might have had to endure unexpected jolts while riding in a horse-drawn coach.

The five hundred pieces of rare porcelain displayed in the Belvedere, were painstakingly acquired within the past quarter century by Dr. Winfried Baer, curator of the Charlottenburg Palace. However, they represent only a fraction of the original royal collection, which exceeded 60,000 pieces prior to World War II. While the archives from this vast collection, including the prints, oil paintings, and sketches that were used for numerous designs at KPM were returned to West Germany in the 1960s, almost none of the original china has ever been recovered.

Long before the first porcelain factory was established in Brandenburg-

Prussia, Chinese and Japanese porcelain was held in high esteem, and was collected by the Great Elector (1640–1688), who had been educated in the Netherlands. Prussia's first Queen Sophie Charlotte (1688–1705) increased the collection, as did Queen Sophie Dorothea (1713–1757), the mother of Frederick the Great. At her death, the latter's Monbijou Palace contained 6,000 East Asian imports, 3,000 pieces of Meissen, together with a large group of porcelains from Vienna and Paris, all of which were destroyed in World War II.

Frederick the Great, a highly educated aesthete as well as an accomplished militarist, took a keen interest in porcelain, which was further heightened after he conquered Meissen in December 1745 during the second Silesian War. Between battles, he made frequent visits to Albrechtsburg, where the Meissen Manufactory was located, and spent much time observing painters and embossers, as well as the firm's leading artist, Johann Joachim Kändler, from whom he commissioned six lavish dinner services. Recognizing the stellar reputation of Meissen, it didn't take him long to realize the economic advantages of developing his own porcelain manufactory in Prussia.

The first Prussian porcelain factory was established by the Berlin industrialist Wilhelm Caspar Wegely in 1751. Wegely, who had bribed the arcanist at the rival Höchst Manufactory to supply him with the formula for hard-paste porcelain, assured Frederick that he could reproduce pieces whose quality would be comparable to Meissen's at a substantially lower cost. Upon hearing that through the establishment of a factory, he "could attract many people to the country, providing them with nourishment and bread," the Prussian monarch granted Wegely a fifty-year monopoly on the production of porcelain. However, at the start of the Seven Years' War in 1756, the calculating Frederick not only confiscated all porcelain stocks from Meissen, Dresden, and Leipzig, but allowed Karl Heinrich Schimmelman, a rather shady merchant, to sell these holdings in Prussia, thus abrogating his agreement with Wegely. By 1757, the Wegely enterprise had come to an end.

Nonetheless, this initial setback did not deter Frederick from pursuing his overall objective. Before the war was even over in Saxony, he appointed the Berlin financier and art dealer Johann Ernst Gotzkowsky to set up a factory in Berlin to produce Meissen-quality porcelain. He couldn't have chosen a more suitable candidate for the task: Gotzkowsky had not only worked his way up from poverty to become one of the wealthiest men in Prussia, but his artistic discernment was also exceptional. (It was this same Gotzkowsky who had amassed an extraordinary collection of Old

THIS *DÉJEUNER*, PACKED IN ITS ORIGINAL
RED MOROCCO LEATHER CASE,
MANAGED TO SURVIVE THE UNEXPECTED JOLTS
THAT WERE FREQUENT WHEN RIDING IN A HORSE-DRAWN COACH.

Masters, which were later sold to Catherine the Great when Frederick was unable to pay for them. Today, they form the nucleus of the painting collection at Saint Petersburg's Hermitage Museum.)

Gotzkowsky did not even wait for the war to end before he set up the new porcelain factory in Berlin. In addition to hiring a number of talented artists from Wegely's defunct operation, he also was able to lure a number of important artists away from Meissen's manufactory by promising them higher salaries. Although the firm got off to a promising start, it barely survived a year, due largely to Gotzkowsky's disastrous currency speculations, which ruined him entirely. "Within two days Frederick bought the entire manufactory with his own funds at the very high price of 225,000 Thalers," notes Dr. Ilse Baer, KPM Archives (Land Berlin). "The pieces that he acquired—there are only about 100 pieces in existence—are regarded as the rarest in the history of Berlin porcelain." Seeing the exquisite harmony between the porcelain's molded shapes, gilding, and painted decoration, as well as the unusually delicate and playful charm of Gotzkowsky's ceramic figurines, one understands why this period porcelain is so prized today.

Berlin's third porcelain factory, known as the Königliche Porzellan Manufaktur (KPM) was the private property of the king. There is probably no other monarch who took such an intense interest in the affairs of a factory as did Frederick the Great. He not only involved himself in the problems of construction, technical improvements, as well as all aspects of form and quality, he even established detailed rules for the training and qualification of his workers. The dinner services produced by the KPM under the monarch's aegis were exceptional, due in part to his commissions, which were sometimes based on his own detailed designs.

Much to his disappointment, Frederick proved to be his own best customer, especially during KPM's early years. By the time of his death, he had purchased 200,000 Thalers worth of porcelain, including twenty-one dinner services for his numerous royal castles and many official gifts. When the king wished to consolidate an alliance, he often did so with a valuable gift of porcelain.

In 1772, he sent Catherine the Great a dessert service for 120 place settings, augmented by a substantial series of figurines—a total of 2,500 pieces. The Czarina was portrayed in luminous white porcelain enthroned under a canopy surrounded by personifications of the arts and sciences and representatives of different Russian ethnic groups, as well as trophies and chained figures commemorating the Russian victory over the Turks. Upon receiving this awesome gift, the Russian empress invited scores of guests to the Hermitage Palace to admire it.

Now, thanks to the splendid exhibition of Berlin porcelain at the Belvedere, we too can share Catherine's wonder and admiration for the beauty and craftsmanship of these antique KPM services.

THIS NEOCLASSICAL SERVICE IS DECORATED WITH IMITATION FLORENTINE AND
ROMAN MOSAICS AND SEMI-PRECIOUS STONES, SUCH AS ROSE QUARTZ AND LAPIS LAZULI.
(PHOTO: STIFTUNG PREUSSISCHE SCHLÖSSER UND GÄRTEN BERLIN-BRANDENBURG,
SCHLOSS CHARLOTTENBURG, FOTOTHEK)

Botanical Museum Berlin-Dahlem

Freie Universität Berlin
Königin-Luise-Strasse 6–8
14191 Berlin
Tel: 83006–0

Open Tuesday through Sunday
10:00 A.M. to 5:00 P.M.

S-Bahn: 1 to Rathaus Steglitz,
then take Bus 183 to the end of
Grunewaldstrasse.

DECORATIVE AND PRACTICAL AT ONCE,
THE TWO TOWERS
ON THIS UNIQUE GABLE-FRONT
ART NOUVEAU GREENHOUSE CONTAIN
SPIRAL STAIRCASES.

WHEN the Egyptian Pharaoh Ramses II (1292–1225 B.C.) was being prepared for burial in the tomb, his attendants showered the coffin with flowers as part of the sepulchral offerings that were intended to accompany him on his journey to the underworld. Considering the average life span of flowers, it is all the more remarkable to see the dried remains of floral garlands, leaves, and petals from the king's tomb, now on display at the Botanical Museum in Berlin's Dahlem district.

Visitors who have the opportunity to discover this unusual and informative museum, one of the most interesting of its kind in Europe, may also be surprised to learn that it contains some of the oldest food samples in the world—grains of emmer (a precursor of wheat), malted barley (used for brewing beer), grape leaves, and fruits from the date-palm and fig-tree (c. 2000 B.C.)—as well as scraps of ancient linen mummy wrappings made from flax, and fragments of papyrus texts (c. 3500 B.C.).

These ancient vegetal remains, which are among the museum's most valuable exhibits, were discovered and donated to the museum by the remarkable German botanist and explorer Georg Schweinfurth (1836–1925), who devoted his life to independent scholarship, even producing a Hebrew-Arabic-Ethiopian dictionary. "Because he collected what other archaeologists threw away, he was able to amass the world's largest collection of ancient Egyptian plant specimens," notes Professor Walter Lack, the museum's director. "His most astonishing find was the

IN THE CACTUS GREENHOUSE, THE NEW WORLD SUCCULENTS
HAVE ASTONISHING ROTUND AND COLUMNAR SHAPES.
THE GOLDEN BARREL CACTUS IN THE FOREGROUND WAS FIRST DISCOVERED
AND IMPORTED FROM MEXICO IN 1885 BY BERLIN CACTUS EXPERT
HEINRICH HILDMANN.

skins taken from the imported bulbs of the Ethiopian lily, discovered on the eyeballs of the Egyptian Princess Nessi Chonsu, presumably intended to protect her eyelids from wrinkling after burial!"

It is a miracle that these exceedingly rare vegetal remains are still in the Botanical Museum, considering that on March 1, 1943, the building containing the library and most of the precious herbarium of pressed and

THIS SCALE MODEL OF A DESERT LANDSCAPE
WAS PAINSTAKINGLY CREATED BY BOTANISTS IN THE 1930S.

dried plants, was bombed during the first major Allied air attack on Berlin. If botanists and scholars have dubbed this event "the Dahlem Disaster," it is understandable: prior to the bombing, the institution boasted an herbarium that had grown to encompass four million specimens, placing it on a par with plant collections in Leningrad, Paris, and Kew. "It was the greatest loss to botany in the world," maintains Lack. "It's hard to calculate all that was destroyed, except to say that it was millions of specimens."

Fortunately, some of the most inestimable parts of the herbarium were saved, including over 20,000 plant species amassed by Carl Ludwig Willdenow, the University of Berlin's first professor of botany and one of the first directors of Berlin's Botanical Garden. The half-million specimens that were recovered after the bombing became the core of the new herbarium, which today, thanks to generous gifts, purchases, and exchanges, has grown to include three million pressed and dried plants, including algae, fungi, lichens, mosses, and ferns, making this collection among one of the fifteen largest in the world.

In his 1827 textbook on botany, the German poet and explorer Adelbert von Chamisso summarized the vital importance of the herbarium: "The herbarium is his [the botanist's] living memory in which he keeps nature ready to view, to compare and to examine at any time." His statement is still valid today: only through the repeated "view" of different specimens is it possible to acquire comprehensive knowledge of the plant world's history and diversity— invaluable data for researchers working in such diverse fields as conservation, agronomy, and bioengineering.

State-of-the-art research tools

THIS EXHIBIT DEMONSTRATES THE VITAL ROLE THE WIND, INSECTS, AND BIRDS PLAY IN POLLINATION.

permit botanists to date plant life on earth millions of years ago. By using gold isotopes, botanists were able to confirm that the museum's oldest fossilized plant specimen, the *Rhynia major*, discovered inside a hard siliceous rock in Rhynie, Scotland, was 395 million years old!

The Botanical Museum, which was first established in 1879 in Schöneberg before moving to its present site early in this century, complements the adjacent Botanical Garden in presenting highlights of the history of botanical research (with an emphasis on German botanists), as well as photos, dioramas, and models of plants, flowers, and morphological details, often invisible to the naked eye.

This highly didactic museum, which is part of an internationally acclaimed research institution, appeals to both school-age children and specialists, with its displays showing

the role of wind, bees, beetles, night-moths, flies, and birds in cross-pollination, or the unexpected similarities between the ordinary onion and the insect-eating pitcher plant.

Not to be overlooked are the exhibits showing the origin of cultivated plants and the examples of products derived from them, including oils, spices, fibers, and wood. For instance, maize, the precursor of corn, was first grown in Mexico six thousand years ago. Archaeological findings confirm that this plant did not evolve naturally, as was once presumed, but was a hybrid devised by the American Indians through the crossbreeding of numerous generations of native American grasses. In fact, the immediate progenitor of corn was a grass called "teosinte" known to later Mexican Indians as *madre de maize* ("mother of corn"). "Botanists now believe maize began to be cultivated when the Indians realized that even the smallest, hardest kernels (characteristic of early corn), popped like popcorn when they were cooked over a fire," Dr. Lack notes.

The museum also presents an interesting overview of the origins and development of the botanical garden, which is as much a place of research and study, as a verdant and fragrant showplace in the center of a steel, concrete, and glass metropolis. Medicinal herb gardens, first cultivated in monasteries and hospices during the Middle Ages, are the precursors of the botanic gardens that were first established in the sixteenth century at the universities of Pisa, Padua, and Bologna. These gardens were used by medical students to gain knowledge about healing plants. In fact, the word botany comes from the Greek word *botanon*, meaning herbal lore.

The Swedish botanist and taxonomist Carolus Linnaeus (1707–1778) developed the first systematized plant sections in botanical gardens, as well as the first system of plant classification. An enlarged facsimile of a beautifully illustrated chart outlining his classification of the plant kingdom according to male and female components, is prominently displayed in the museum's botanical history section. In drawing up his system, Linnaeus used a single characteristic—the number of "sexual organs" in flowers—which he regarded as the most important facet of any plant, even those not yet discovered. Although he aroused the Vatican's indignation by using this analogy to explain his theory, his system was nonetheless quickly accepted.

While this classification system is no longer valid today, Linnaeus's invention of binomial nomenclature (every living organism is given a generic name in which the species is classified, followed by an additional word, unique to the species), is still used to label all biological species, including plants. The term *Homo sapiens* ("wise man" in Latin) defining the human species, was introduced by Linnaeus.

Berlin has had a botanical garden for over three hundred years. In 1646, the Hohenzollern Great Elector Friederich Wilhelm commissioned the Lustgarten opposite the Berlin City Palace, which was planted with rare shrubs and trees. By 1679, a model agricultural garden had been laid out in Schöneberg, on the grounds of the present-day Kleist Park. Over the next two centuries, this garden would evolve into a scientifically acclaimed botanical garden planted with specimens from the four corners of the globe. Among its marvels was the giant Amazon water lily *(Victoria amazonica)*, which required the building of a separate greenhouse.

The present botanical garden in Dahlem, adjacent to the museum, was laid out between 1897 and 1903; Germany's belated acquisition of African colonies necessitated research into tropical crops, and the garden at Schöneberg lacked the acreage to build more greenhouses for this purpose. Although devastated during World War II, the present 126-acre botanical garden (which boasts over 20,000 different plant species), has regained its former magnificence. Besides its sixteen greenhouses devoted primarily to the raising and study of Mediterreanean and tropical plants, its renowned Geographical Section offers an incomparable botanical tour around the world that begins with the vegetation of Europe, including German forests, swamp, and aquatic plants, then proceeds across miniature mountain ranges, from the Pyrenees and the Alps to the

THIS GIANT MODEL OF A MAGNOLIA FLOWER IS MADE OF RESIN AND TOOK OVER TWO YEARS TO BUILD, AT A COST OF $250,000.

Carpathian Mountains and the Himalayas, and then completes the journey with the flora of Northeast Asia, South Africa, China and Japan, and the Americas.

The Botanical Museum and the adjacent Botanical Garden represent a wonderful amalgam of scientific research and natural beauty, offering visitors an illuminating presentation of our biosphere and its mysteries, while underscoring botany's vital role in our lives. A tour of this museum reminds us just how rich and fragile our environment is, and that it behooves us to know it well in order to better preserve it.

Brecht House-Brecht-Weigel Memorial

Chausseestrasse 125
10115 Berlin
Tel: 282–99–16

Open only for half-hour guided tours (maximum eight persons) Tuesday, Wednesday, and Friday 10:00 A.M. to 11:30 A.M. Thursday 10:00 A.M. to 11:30 A.M. and 5:00 P.M. to 6:30 P.M. Saturday 9:30 A.M. to 1:30 P.M. The memorial rooms are closed on public holidays.

U-Bahn: 6 to Oranienburger Tor
S-Bahn: 1 to Friedrichstrasse
Tram: 1, 13
Bus: 140, 157

IN March 1954, the German playwright and poet Bertholt Brecht (1888–1956) wrote to his publisher Peter Suhrkamp: "I'm now living in Chausseestrasse, next to the 'French' graveyard, where Huguenot generals and Hegel and Fichte are buried; all my windows look out on the cemetery grounds. I have three rooms on the first floor of the back building, which like the front building is said to be about a hundred-and-fifty years old. The rooms are high and so are the windows, which have pleasant proportions. The largest room is about nine meters square, so I can put in several desks for different jobs. Actually the whole place is well-proportioned, it's really a good idea to live in houses and with furniture that are at least a hundred-and-twenty years old, let's say, in early capitalist surroundings until later socialist surroundings are available."

The telling nature of this letter becomes apparent to the visitor who has the opportunity to take a guided tour of the Brecht-Weigel House, where little has changed since one of Germany's most famous and controversial authors was in residence. The "early capitalist surroundings" are an apt description for Brecht's tastefully furnished, book-lined spacious rooms, decorated with valuable Chinese scrolls, striking

BERTHOLT BRECHT SPENT THE LAST YEARS OF HIS LIFE IN A COMFORTABLE, SECOND-FLOOR APARTMENT IN THIS 1840 BUILDING, ENJOYING COMFORTS AND PRIVILEGES THAT WERE UNAVAILABLE TO ORDINARY EAST GERMAN CITIZENS.

THE MEETING ROOM OVERLOOKS A GARAGE
WHERE BRECHT USED TO KEEP HIS CAR, A BMW—HIS OWNERSHIP OF
SUCH A LUXURIOUS ITEM WAS CAREFULLY CONCEALED
FROM THE CITIZENS OF THE FORMER EAST GERMAN COMMUNIST REGIME.

Noh theater masks, and handsome Biedermeier antiques. Even if Brecht persisted in conveying an impression to the world at large of his staunch pro-Marxist sympathies, and cultivated a proletarian look with his worker's cap and deceptively simple, custom-tailored clothes, his last home reveals that his status as a member of the Left-wing intelligentsia entitled him to such special perks as this sizeable, comfortable apartment which, under ordinary circumstances then, might have been shared by several families. Unlike his fellow East Germans, he enjoyed a munificent salary (more than ten times the average worker's monthly pay), drove a luxurious BMW, and always had a ready supply of cigars, as well as a servant, at his disposal.

It was in this rented, second-floor apartment built around 1840 that Brecht was to spend the last years of his life, occupied with the direction of his own theatrical troupe, the Berliner Ensemble, which was dedicated essentially to performing his own dramatic works. He was in the habit of rising daily at 6:00 A.M. and writing until 10:00 A.M., before rehearsals began at the theater. The apartment's large, bright study also permitted discussions and conferences with Brecht's rather large circle of friends and colleagues, pupils, and theater staff. Many texts were written at the residence in Chausseestrasse, including poetry, prose works, essays on artistic and political topics, as well as his famous *Open Letter to the West German Bundestag* opposing the reintroduction of compulsory military service. (While Brecht repeatedly castigated the Western democracies, he was rather reluctant to challenge any policies or actions taken by his hosts, including the use of Soviet tanks to crush the 1953 workers' rebellion.)

His constant companion was the actress Helene Weigel, his second wife (whom he had married in 1929, and who occupied the apartment above his, beginning in January 1954). From the end of 1956 until her death in 1971, she lived on the ground floor of the building, in simply furnished rooms that included a glassed-in plant-filled veranda. (These rooms have now been restored and are also open to the public.)

It was after her husband's death that Helene Weigel founded the Bertolt Brecht Archive, which undertook the classification and safeguarding of Brecht's notebooks, manuscripts, and journals, copies of which are housed in her former apartment on the second floor. (The originals, which are kept in a safe, were acquired from Brecht's three surviving children by the City of Berlin at the end of 1992 for the staggering sum of eleven million tax-free DM.)

During his lifetime, Brecht was primarily known as a playwright and theatrical director. Under the influence of Erwin Piscator's proletarian theater and Karl Marx's theories of dialectical materialism, Brecht broke with the theatrical establishment and developed a primarily narrative style with a direct political message, which came to be known as "epic theater." With his exotic stage settings, flat lighting, and unrealistic scenery, his intention was to deter the audience from becoming emotionally involved, thereby inciting a more critical analysis of the action on stage. Subjecting his actors to lengthy and demanding rehearsals, Brecht often proved to be a challenging director. Nonetheless, he succeeded in striking up remarkable partnerships with talented composers whose contributions

BRECHT'S BLACK MANUAL TYPEWRITER AND SOLID OAK WRITING DESK ARE NEXT TO A WINDOW OVERLOOKING THE DOROTHEENSTADT CEMETERY, WHERE THE PLAYWRIGHT AND HIS WIFE, HELENE WEIGEL, ARE NOW BURIED.

THE LIBRARY CONTAINS OVER FOUR THOUSAND BOOKS
IN BOTH PAPERBACK AND HARDCOVER EDITIONS.
ALTHOUGH BRECHT MAINTAINED THAT HIS FAVORITE AUTHORS INCLUDED
SOPHOCLES, HORACE, SHAKESPEARE, WILLIAM FAULKNER, AND WALT WHITMAN,
HE WAS ALSO AN AVID READER OF PAPERBACK MYSTERIES.

did a great deal to establish his subsequent reputation. The first and most celebrated was Kurt Weill, with whom he collaborated on the musical *The Little Mahoganny* (1927), the enormously successful *The Threepenny Opera* (1928), which updated John Gay's *The Beggar's Opera* as well as the poetry of the French troubadour-poet François Villon, followed later by the musical *Happy End* (1929).

Critical opinion now tends to attribute the continued popularity of these musical scores more to Weill's unforgettable melodies than to the power of Brecht's texts. After the playwright's falling-out with Weill (who couldn't stomach his collaborator's doctrinaire politics), Brecht worked with Hanns Eisler, who shared his political beliefs. (Eisler, an avowed Communist, wrote the music for the national anthem of the former German Democratic Republic.)

Brecht—who left Germany the day after the Reichstag fire—is said to have produced his best work during his fifteen years in exile, when he moved successively from Switzerland to Denmark, Soviet Russia, and California. Returning to East Berlin in 1948, with the government's guarantee that a theater would be placed at his disposal, the playwright and his wife rapidly acquired a major international following for their Berliner Ensemble, which they began in 1949. Among the theatrical troupe's legendary performances were productions of Brecht's *Mother Courage and Her Children*, *The Caucasian Chalk Circle*, and *Senora Carrar's Rifles*—all with Helene Weigel in the lead female roles.

As one of the few prominent intellectuals who had chosen voluntarily to live in the new Communist state, Brecht enjoyed a privileged status as one of the country's leading celebrities. However, knowing the tragic fate of some of his former collaborators (who were victims of Stalin's purges), before moving to East Germany he

works were not only criticized by the East German cultural authorities, but were often greeted with incomprehension and organized silence.

Although there were more than eighty productions of Brecht's plays mounted worldwide during 1998

BRECHT'S SPARTAN BEDROOM STILL CONTAINS HIS CHARACTERISTIC WORKER'S CAP AND WALKING STICK, AS WELL AS AN ANTIQUE CHINESE SCROLL, WHICH INSPIRED ONE OF HIS MOST FAMOUS POEMS, *THE DOUBTER*.

took the precaution of acquiring Austrian citizenship. He also maintained the copyright for his works with a West German publisher in order to assure a hard-currency income that could be transferred to a Swiss bank account.

Despite the generous subsidies given to the Berliner Ensemble and the Soviet Union's endorsement (in 1955 the playwright was awarded the Stalin Prize, worth $250,000), Brecht's productions were not always lauded by the GDR's cultural hardliners. Although initially received with enthusiasm, Brecht's later staged

(the hundredth anniversary of his birth), in recent years the playwright's reputation has been subject to major shifts in critical opinion both within Germany and beyond her borders. Once hailed as being among the twentieth century's great artistic innovators, who shaped the direction of drama and theatrical productions, more recently he has been accused of misogyny, anti-Semitism, and plagiarism, as well as moral and political cowardice.

His standing has not only been tarnished by the failure and collapse of Communism, whose cause he championed in most of his work, but also by the recent publication of John Fuegi's myth-shattering biography *The Life and Lies of Bertolt Brecht*, in which he shows that Brecht's written contribution to his own oeuvre was comparatively slim. The dramatic

growing up, Brecht was presented as a Socialist hero," she notes. "They didn't say that he had an Austrian passport, nor that he was a philanderer, nor that he collaborated a lot with various women. We were told that all the work came from his pen. They

HELENE WEIGEL'S PLANT-FILLED GARDEN ROOM STILL CONTAINS HER COLLECTION OF ANTIQUE SILVER SPOONS AND MEISSEN CHINA.

works that had made Brecht a cultural icon had, in fact, been largely written by other writers, notably Elisabeth Hauptmann, Grete Steffin, and Ruth Berlau. Although all three women were at one time his lovers, as well as dedicated collaborators, not one of them ever received appropriate recognition, nor a fraction of the royalties that made Brecht an extremely wealthy man.

In light of such revelations, Elke Pfeil, director of the Brecht-Weigel Memorial (who grew up in the GDR), has had to revise her own notions of Brecht. "When I was

didn't even say that he liked cars and that he owned a BMW. They made him out to be far less human than he truly was."

Pfeil believes the restoration of Brecht House and the Brecht-Weigel Archive now gives scholars and other visitors a more balanced insight into the author's legacy. "Now, when people come here, they have a chance to understand his whole life, including his political inclinations, and to see a whole person." No artist, not even a Bertholt Brecht, could have hoped for more.

Bröhan Museum

Schlosstrasse la
14059 Berlin-Charlottenburg
Tel: 321–40–29

Open Tuesday through Sunday
10:00 A.M. to 6:00 P.M.

U-Bahn: 7 to Richard Wagner
Platz
Bus: 109, 110, 145, X26

THE BRÖHAN MUSEUM IS LOCATED
IN A REMODELED NEOCLASSICAL GARRISON
OPPOSITE THE CHARLOTTENBURG PALACE.

D URING the five decades between the Paris Universal Exhibitions of 1889 and 1937, France, Belgium, Germany, Austria, and Scandinavia witnessed an unprecedented flowering in the fields of applied art and industrial design encompassing home furnishings, porcelain, glass-making, and metal-work in silver and pewter. From this period came two unprecedented artistic movements that broke with the nineteenth century's historicism and Victoriana—Art Nouveau, which emphasized curvilinear, organic plant forms, and Art Deco, which featured spare, elegant designs using the finest in materials and workmanship.

In German-speaking countries, Art Nouveau came to be known as *Jugendstil*, after a magazine called *Die Jugend* that popularized the style. To mark this aesthetic break with the past, a *Secessionhaus* was built in Vienna in the new "Secession" style to exhibit works by ground-breaking artists, and decorated with this euphoric inscription: *'Der Zeit Ihre Kunst: Der Kunst Ihre Freiheit'* (Art for its time; freedom for its Art).

However, not everyone applauded this clamor for artistic freedom and self-expression. Germany's Kaiser Wilhelm II held very different views regarding art: "Art that transgresses the laws and perimeters which I lay down ceases to be art. The misused word 'liberty' leads to licence and presumption. If art is to fulfill its proper role, it must affect people deeply—but it must be uplifting and not degrading." From this turmoil over "acceptable" art sprang the Berlin Secession movement in 1892,

THESE ART NOUVEAU TEAPOTS WITH WARMERS IN SILVER, BRASS, AND COPPER
WERE MADE BY GERMAN, FRENCH, ENGLISH, AND DUTCH CRAFTSMEN.

led by the painters Max Liebermann, Walter Lestikow, Frank Skarbina, Lesser Uri, Hans Baluschek, and Käthe Kollwitz—a movement that was to have as much of an impact on the century as Art Nouveau and Art Deco.

The Bröhan Museum's collection demonstrates that art and home furnishings once thought to be alien and unacceptable, are now regarded as ground-breaking and notable. Since October 1983, the public has been able to admire this outstanding collection of Art Nouveau and Art Deco furniture, glass, ceramics, silver,

THESE ART NOUVEAU DINING-ROOM TABLE, CHAIRS, SIDEBOARD, AND DISH CABINET
WERE MADE BY HECTOR GUIMARD IN 1898.
(GUIMARD IS BEST REMEMBERED FOR DESIGNING THE WROUGHT-IRON ENTRANCES
TO THE PARIS METRO.)

and Secessionist paintings, thanks to a munificent gift to the City of West Berlin by Professor Karl H. Bröhan on the occasion of his sixtieth birthday.

Nonetheless, it remains one of the city's best kept secrets. The serenity and quiet of its handsomely appointed furnished rooms makes for a welcome respite from Berlin's other crowded museums and palaces, and provides a suitable environment for contemplating the stunning craftsmanship of such notable talents as Hector Guimard, Louis Marjorelle, Emile Gallé, Paul Iribe, Jacques Emile Ruhlmann, and Josef Hoffmann. Rounding out the collection are works by the Luminarist landscape painter Karl Hagemeister (1848–1933), the Social Realist Hans Baluschek (1870–1935), who has been compared with Toulouse-

Lautrec, the Naturalist painter Willy Jaekel (1888–1944), and the Cubist painter and sculptor Jean-Lambert Rucki (1888–1967), all founding members of the Berlin Secession.

Although initially drawn to eighteenth-century porcelain from Berlin's Royal Manufactory (his extensive collection now forms the bulk of the porcelain collection at the Belvedere in the Charlottenburg Palace complex), Bröhan became enamored with Art Nouveau after seeing the 1966 exhibition *Werke um 1900* (Works around 1900) at the Berlin Kunstgewerbe Museum. Gradually acquiring knowledge about this period, he began an intensive search for Art Nouveau and Art Deco objects that eventually culminated in a collection of several thousand objects. "My motto was a quotation from the German philosopher

Goethe, 'Taste is formed by the most excellent, not the mediocre.' Our aim is to show that different expressions of art can be of equal value," he says. "Is not a glass designed by Wilhelm Wagenbach for serial production equal to a painting of good quality? Our aim is to demonstrate that at this museum."

Visitors are able to gain an excellent overview of Art Nouveau and Art Deco design from the museum's period rooms, which are furnished with the work of French cabinetmakers featured in the 1900 and 1925 international Paris exhibitions. These Art Nouveau and Art Deco pieces of furniture were luxurious objects created with the most precious woods for members of European high society, who had both taste and the money to indulge it. This furniture followed the great tradition in cabinetry established within the court of Louis XIV, which had been marked by the creations of such renowned designers as Boulle, Oeben, Riesener, and Jacob.

The museum boasts a fine grouping of Art Nouveau flower-ornamented furniture, glassware, and porcelain of Emile Gallé (1846–1904) and his colleagues from Nancy, as well as the curvilinear furniture carried by the well-known Parisian art dealer Siegfried Bing, whose Parisian gallery La Maison de l'Art Nouveau gave the art movement its name. Gallé's versatile artistry (he was a ceramicist, glassmaker, and furniture designer) is demonstrated in his naturalistic cabinets, which often boast exquisite floral marquetry patterns made of native fruitwoods and exotic hardwoods, and sometimes quotations worked in intarsia. A particularly exquisite étagère is inlaid with a passage in Latin from *The Sermon on the Mount*, "Blessed are the meek for they shall inherit the earth."

Gallé's experiments with painting colored enamels on glass, as well as his studies of his native plant world, provided him with the technique and subject matter to create some of the most stunning glassware of this century. During the 1880s, he developed his mature style: instead of working with clear or transparently tinted glass, he used a vitreous mass consisting of several opaquely colored layers with cameo work applied in relief. This laborious technique consisted of melting pre-formed pieces of glass into a heated vitreous mass which, after solidifying and undergoing an engraving process, formed brightly colored flowers or butterflies. One stunning vase reveals his knowledge of botany; made of differentiated shades of green and brown enamel inlays that resemble a clump of moss,

delicate fern-like leaves and umbels with spherical clusters of flowers are discernible. A slate-gray lifelike moth, modeled onto the smooth side of the vase, rests on the blossoms.

Parisian Art Nouveau did not just emulate the outer forms of nature, but strove to create in abstract organic structures—be they in metal, porcelain, or wood. The greatest practitioner of this type of design was the architect Hector Guimard, who is best remembered for his picturesque wrought-iron entrances to the Paris Metro. The museum boasts an elegant fruitwood Guimard dining-room set consisting of a buffet, a table, and dining-chairs, notable for their sinuous lines that impart an unexpected lightness and dynamism.

The outstanding personality of French cabinetry to emerge after World War I was the Alsatian Jacques-Emile Ruhlmann, who has been called the "Riesener of the twentieth

THE VERSATILE CARTOONIST AND FASHION DESIGNER, PAUL IRIBE,
CREATED THESE EBONY AND VELVET-UPHOLSTERED ARMCHAIRS IN 1914.
THE PAINTINGS ARE BY THE FRENCH CUBIST JEAN-LAMBERT RUCKI (1888–1967).

century," an apt comparison when one considers that he used only the most precious materials (such as ebony, mahogany, and ivory) and maintained the highest standards of craftsmanship to create perfectly proportioned furniture. Such elegance came at a price, of course: the average annual income of an academic was barely sufficient to pay for a dressing-table. However, the elitist Ruhlmann was persuaded that only the upper classes, with their substantial resources, could pave the way for new art movements.

He also had his share of emulators, including the Parisian cabinetmaker Jules Leleu, and the furniture of the Parisian firm Dominique. Among the museum's outstanding pieces are a woman's secretaire made of birch-wood with a sharkskin blotter by Dominique (c. 1925), and a Leleu armoire whose doors are decorated with iridescent mother-of-pearl inlays.

The era's elegance is further confirmed by the museum's outstanding silverware from Paris and Copenhagen, notably from the Danish silversmith Georg Jensen (1866–1935) and the French gold-and-silversmith Jean Puiforcat. While Jensen's earliest work reflected the floral Art Nouveau style, he and his collaborators Johan Rohde, Harald Nielsen, and Sigvard Bernadotte (the son of the Swedish king Gustav Adolph VI), were soon gaining recognition for their remarkably plain and unadorned silverwork. They demonstrated that excellent new designs, which emphasized restrained elegance and harmonious propor-tions, were the means of confirming Jensen's stellar reputation.

Jean Puiforcat, who trained as a sculptor, received critical acclaim even for his earliest works, which tended to be square cut and angular, instead of the traditional round shape.

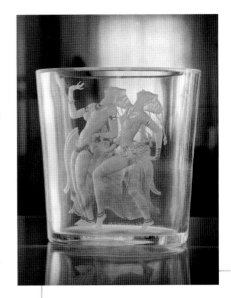

THIS ETCHED CRYSTAL VASE OF EXOTIC DANCERS (C. 1930) DESIGNED BY EDWARD HALD FOR ORREFORS, THE SWEDISH CRYSTAL MANUFACTURER, IS AN OUTSTANDING EXAMPLE OF INTAGLIO ENGRAVING.

Fascinated by the perfect smoothness and gleaming coolness of modern technology, Puiforcat refrained from hammering, then held in high esteem by fellow artists as a mark of craftsmanship. Eventually his work became an unattainable ideal for other French silversmiths, who were inspired by Puiforcat's high quality and originality.

Thanks to the passion and erudition of Professor Bröhan, visitors to this elegant museum can now discover the unique talents that inspired and developed two outstand-ing periods in design, as well as admire some of the less-well-known artists of the Berlin Secession. His unerring eye proves that various art forms once viewed as strange and forbidding, can now be appreciated as high points in formal beauty.

The Bridge Museum-Berlin

Bussardsteig 9
D-14195 Berlin (Dahlem)
Tel: 8–31–20–29 or 8–32–60–12

Open Wednesday through Monday
11:00 A.M. to 5:00 P.M.
Open New Year's Day
1:00 P.M. to 5:00 P.M.

U-Bahn: 1 to Oskar Helene-Heim,
then Bus 115 to
Clayallee/Pücklerstrasse

"BELIEVING in a new generation of those who create and those who enjoy, we call all young people together, and as young people who carry the future in us, we want to wrest freedom for our gestures and for our lives from the older, comfortably established forces. We claim as our own everyone who reproduces directly and without falsification whatever it is that drives him to create."

Such was the manifesto that Ernst Ludwig Kirchner drafted and engraved on wood for *Die Brücke* or *The Bridge*, a German artists' group active in Dresden and Berlin from

THE WHITE CONCRETE, FLAT-ROOFED DIE BRÜCKE MUSEUM
AT THE EDGE OF THE GRUNEWALD FOREST
WAS BUILT AT THE INITIATIVE OF THE ARTIST KARL SCHMIDT-ROTTLUFF,
WHO LEFT MANY OF HIS WORKS TO THE CITY OF BERLIN.

1905 to 1914, which rebelled against the stifling academicism of Wilhelmine Germany. Pioneered by four architectural students from the Technical University of Dresden, Ernst Ludwig Kirchner, Erich Heckel, Karl Schmidt-Rottluff, and Fritz Bleyl, who would later be joined by Max Pechstein, Emil Nolde, and Otto Mueller, the style of painting and graphic artwork of the Die Brücke group became associated with flat, linear, rhythmic drawing and a daring simplification of form and color. Inspired by the tormented art of the Norwegian painter Edvard Munch and the passionate intensity of Vincent van Gogh, as well as by primitive Polynesian and African statuary, this early form of Expressionism reflected a powerful disinclination to follow traditional avenues.

"They brought a frenzied dedication to their painting and tolerated no instruction," explains Dr. Wolf-Dieter Dube in *The Expressionists.* "They wanted to preserve the freshness and naïveté of their sensations, the strength and honesty of their visions. Their self-will and self-confidence, the uncompromisingly high demands they made on themselves and on the world in general, gave them the power to set up their own goals and to reject both traditional ideals and traditional skills."

The members of the Brücke also set themselves apart from other artistic groups by inviting the public to become "passive members" of their group. For an annual subscription of twelve marks, these members— some of whom were extremely active in promoting an understanding and appreciation of this new kind of art—

THESE NUDES, PORTRAITS, STILL-LIFES, AND SEASCAPE
REVEAL BOTH THE STRIKING VERSATILITY,
AS WELL AS A CERTAIN CONTINUITY OF STYLE,
IN THE WORK OF DIE BRÜCKE.

THE HARSH, ABBREVIATED
FORMAL LANGUAGE OF DIE BRÜCKE
IS EXPRESSED IN THIS ETCHING
BY ERICH HECKEL (1908),
TITLED *FISHERWOMAN*.
(PHOTO: BRÜCKE-MUSEUM BERLIN)

received a report each year outlining the group's activities and a portfolio of prints, the "Brücke-Mappen" (Bridge Portfolio), which eventually became quite valuable. Sixty-eight such members were recruited in this fashion.

Visitors to the shimmering glass and white concrete, flat-roofed Bauhaus-inspired Die Brücke Museum at the edge of the Grunewald Forest, now have the opportunity to discover this early and urbane manifestation of Expressionism. Built by Werner Düttmann between 1966 and 1967 at the initiative of the artist Karl Schmidt-Rottluff (1884–1976), the museum presents a collection of some four hundred paintings, sculptures, and graphic works by the artists associated with this group, including a substantial number by its two

co-founders, Heckel and Schmitt-Rottluff, who not only bequeathed a larger part of their *oeuvre* to the city, but also contributed to financing the museum's construction. Rounding out the collection are a superb selection of oils, watercolors, and sculptures by Kirchner, Mueller, and Pechstein.

Among the works in the collection are a number depicting a celebration of the harmony between man and nature, characteristic of the group's early period in Dresden and Moritzberg. During this time, the artists worked and lived collectively, doing carefree work in a natural setting that suggested a flight from civilization. Their principal subjects were nudes in landscape settings, presented as just another aspect of nature, as well as the circus and music-hall.

In order to free themselves from entrenched bourgeois attitudes toward art, the group aimed to subordinate the individual to the general, even going so far as to eliminate specific names or other personal attributes in the titles of their pictures. The sketches and watercolors from this period, notably those by Kirchner, Pechstein, and Schmidt-Rottluff, reveal a surprising spontaneity of expression, which arose from drawing nudes quickly.

When *Die Brücke's* members moved to Berlin in 1911, in the hope of attaining a more secure financial footing, they abandoned their radiant color scheme and pastoral themes for a darker palette that portrayed the ambiguous and alienating aspects of the teaming metropolis. Kirchner's 1913 *Berlin Street Scene,* with its sharp forms and nervous, rapid brush strokes depicting a crowd of haughty coquettes and men in black homburgs and dark blue overcoats, captures the demoralizingly mood of the city.

The museum also boasts a fine selection of works by Emil Nolde, an artist who proved as talented as Kirchner, but whose solitariness and individualism prevented him from remaining within the Brücke's confines for more than eighteen months. Taking external reality as his starting point, he painted portraits, landscapes, and garden scenes, using a brilliant palette that "transformed nature by infusing it with one's own mind and spirit." In 1909, barely recovered from a serious illness, Nolde was seized with a fierce desire to paint profound religious and spiritual works, whose visionary mood emanates almost entirely from dazzling color and light, a technique that is strikingly exemplified in *The Mocking of Christ*.

Still, it was not through painting, but through the woodcut that the artists of *Die Brücke* attained their highest degree of artistic development. In their search for the most direct and economical formal means of expressing the essence of a subject, Kirchner, Heckel, Pechstein, and Schmidt-Rottluff made the woodcut their characteristic medium, thereby re-establishing it as a major art form in Germany. Although initially influenced by Art Nouveau, Symbolism, and Japonisme, the group's later works show their tremendous debt to Edvard Munch's disturbing, highly atmospheric graphic work, which is typified in *The Scream*.

Die Brücke's encounters with the art of indigenous tribes at the Dresden Museum of Ethnology, notably from the Palau Islands in the Pacific Ocean, was to have the most decisive impact on the group's graphic arts. Looking back on his career, Kirchner recalled that he found the carved beam of the Palau Indians brought back by a much-

THIS WOODEN SCULPTURE,
THE MAN WITH THE ROUND CAP,
BY KARL SCHMIDT-ROTTLUFF,
REFLECTS THE INFLUENCE OF THE
PRIMITIVE ART OF
THE PALAU ISLANDERS, WHICH HAD A
PROFOUND IMPACT ON THE
ARTISTS OF DIE BRÜCKE.
(PHOTO: BRÜCKE MUSEUM-BERLIN)

acclaimed 1908–10 German expedition (with its over two hundred roughly carved figures) reflected the same formal language as his own carvings. It was to inspire Kirchner and his colleagues to abandon a classical ideal of beauty in favor of an aesthetic that emphasized distorted and angular contours, one which indubitably heightens the intensity and power of their work.

Magdalena Moeller, the museum's curator, maintains that *Die Brücke's* graphic output brought a new vitality to the graphic arts which had not been seen in Germany since the Renaissance. "With the woodcuts of Brücke, German printed graphic work experienced a productive period comparable to that of the early sixteenth century," she writes in *Brücke*. "At that time, artists like Albrecht Dürer and the brothers Sebald and Barthel Beham had also created works of an extraordinary, wide-reaching significance. After this, however, the woodcut gradually sank to the level of popular illustrative graphics. It was the artists of Art Nouveau who first attempted to restore more than a utilitarian function to the woodcut. Brücke, which built upon the initial efforts of Art Nouveau, made the woodcut into an independent means of artistic self-expression once again."

In the euphoria of creating a ground-breaking artistic movement, one that would be highly acclaimed during the Weimar Republic, the artists of *Die Brücke* never imagined the day when their works would be banned in Germany. Yet no sooner had the National Socialist Party been swept into power in 1933, than it began a relentless attack on avant-garde art, starting with Expressionism. Not only was this artistic movement defamed in the infamous "Degenerate Art" exhibition of 1938–41, but many artists' works were removed from public collections. The consequences were devastating for the members of *Die Brücke*: not only were they publicly calumniated by Hitler but they were banned from exhibiting and teaching. Even Emil Nolde, who had originally supported the National Socialist Party in the hope of securing their support, was banned from painting. Others suffered even more—in 1938, after seeing 639 of his works confiscated from various German museums, Ernst Kirchner ended his life.

Today, contemplating the works of this artistic movement in the tranquillity of such a well-appointed museum, one is able to apprehend the importance of these early Expressionists who not only made

a radical break with the past, but also had a decisive impact on the development of twentieth-century literature, music, and cinema, including such works as Robert Wiene's *Cabinet of Dr. Caligari* and Frederick William Murnau's *Nosferatu*. *Die Brücke* even had a powerful influence on post-war German painting, particularly upon the works of Georg Baselitz and Markus Lüpertz, known for their aggressive colors and powerful technique. One might say that *Die Brücke's* ambitious manifesto, which sought to explore new pathways in art, raised intriguing questions about beauty and form and proposed a variety of answers that continue to inspire artists today.

THIS PORTRAIT OF MARCELLA (1910)
BY ERNST LUDWIG KIRCHNER
REVEALS THE INFLUENCE OF SUCH FAUVIST PAINTERS
AS ANDRÉ DERAIN AND HENRI MATISSE.
(PHOTO: BRÜCKE MUSEUM-BERLIN)

Düppel Village Museum

Clauertrasse 11
D-14163 Berlin-Zehlendorf
Tel: 802–66–71

Guided tours Sunday and holidays
10:00 A.M. to 5:00 P.M. (last
admission at 4:00 P.M.)
Thursday 3:00 P.M. to 7:00 P.M.
(last admission at 6:00 P.M.)
April to October
Special group tours also available
throughout the year, including
schools. Call ahead for further
information.

U-Bahn: 1 to Oskar-Helene-Heim
S-Bahn: 1 to Zehlendorf, then
take Bus 115 and get off at
Ludwigsfelder/Clauertrasse

Note: The land on Clauertrasse
was part of the former estate that
Prince Frederick Karl acquired in
1850 and named after the victory
of Düppel in the war between
Prussia and Denmark.

WHILE Sunday may be a traditional day of rest elsewhere in Germany, the same cannot be said for this rural Medieval village in the southern part of Berlin. Here there are no idle hands: under a blue sky and broiling sun, field workers are harvesting wheat and rye, gardeners are gathering medicinal plants and natural dyes from the garden, peasant women are spinning wool from the newly shorn sheep into cloth on a manual loom, beekeepers are gathering honey from hives, while young swineherds feed a new litter of pigs. The potter is busy throwing red and black clay pots that will later be fired in the communal kiln, the blacksmith is making farm implements, and the tarmaker is preparing pine and pitch for tar that will later be used on the wooden wheels of an ox cart.

From a distance, the hamlet's circular wood-and-thatch dwellings and roughly clad denizens remind the visitor of the paintings of Peter Brueghel the Elder, known for his realistic portrayals of the peasantry, diligently engaged in rural activities that illustrate both the harsh demands and the plenitude of the earth. The reconstruction and activities of this village built on the vestiges of a former Medieval settlement are so authentic that even the Flemish painter might have been bemused.

Known as the Düppel Village Museum, this unique open-air museum was reconstructed on the traces of an original settlement, briefly inhabited by Slavs and Germans between 1160 and 1220, and founded about the same time as the city of Berlin. Its vestiges were

THE MEDIEVAL VILLAGE OF DÜPPEL HAS BEEN RECONSTRUCTED ON THE TRACES
OF AN ORIGINAL SETTLEMENT THAT WAS BRIEFLY INHABITED BY SLAVS AND GERMANS
FROM 1160 TO 1220, AROUND THE TIME BERLIN WAS FOUNDED.

inadvertently discovered in 1940 by a young boy searching for shrapnel after a bomb had fallen nearby. Buried in the bomb crater were several pieces of medieval pottery dating from 1200. These fragments were brought to Berlin's Museum of Archaeology where they lay forgotten until 1960, when archaeologists became increasingly interested in the Medieval history of Berlin. Although no mention of this settlement could be found in any documents, the shards of pottery indicated that there had probably been a village on the Machnower Krummes Fenn, in an area near Potsdam and Zehlendorf.

Although the Berlin Wall was still an ominous presence in this area, it did not prevent the undertaking of ambitious archaeological excavations beginning in 1968, which ultimately confirmed the existence of this Medieval village. It proved to be quite a challenge to excavate and date a village that had only been inhabited for such a brief span of time. On the other hand, the site itself was advantageous, since it had been left relatively untouched—the only destruction had been the effects of deep plowing, water drainage, and the placement of two anti-aircraft guns during World War II.

Not satisfied with uncovering a mass of pottery shards that might lie dormant in a Berlin Museum, a non-profit organization ("Fördererkreis des Museumsdorfs Düppel e. V."), comprised of passionate amateurs and scholars, moved to re-create a period village using replicas of Medieval tools, oak from the forests that were cleared during the expansion of Tegel Airport, as well as reeds and willows

THIS THATCH-AND-WOODEN HOUSE STILL UNDER CONSTRUCTION
DEMONSTRATES THE MATERIALS AND TECHNIQUES USED IN BUILDING RURAL HOMES
IN MEDIEVAL GERMANY.

for the thatched roofs.

Between 1160 and 1190, a palisade fence with two entrances surrounded what is presumed to have been a customs barrier between Saxony and Berlin-Brandenburg.

Later, between 1180 and 1220, a horseshoe-shaped village was built in the same location. To add to the overall authenticity, a number of houses have been reconstructed on the actual Medieval building sites uncovered during the excavations.

A tour of the various houses reveals both the domestic appointments and discomforts that Europe's peasantry had to endure well beyond the Middle Ages. Not only were such dwellings dim and windowless—the only air came from a hole in the roof —but the floor was made of compressed clay. To keep the house dry, the walls were covered with waterproof clay. Furnishings were spartan, consisting essentially of stools and wooden benches, which did double duty as beds come nightfall. The fire served as both a source of warmth and fuel for cooking. Typically, part of the house included a wood partition behind which the pigs were kept, since they were fattened at home before being slaughtered and then hung from the roof beams to be smoked overhead. Sometimes, there was room for a millstone which could be used to produce stone-ground flour, or for a loom that could be employed to make cloth during the long winter. Bread is still made and baked in the village's clay communal oven, samples of which are offered to visitors.

Each house in the settlement took about two months to complete, and was erected by the labor of three to four volunteers during the summer. The reeds for the roof came from the

Tegel Lake, and were cut in winter, when the ice was frozen. Every house was made with the same types of wood and iron tools used by the peasantry during the Middle Ages.

While volunteers in the homespun garb of their Medieval forebears demonstrate different handicrafts and techniques, they also show that life in such settlements was always a struggle. Not only were the houses vulnerable to fire and floods, but a poor harvest could result in starvation. Much of the crop that was sown had to be given to the Church and the German Ascanian princes, before any of it could be consumed by the peasantry.

During the Middle Ages and later periods, European agriculture utilized the three-field system of crop rotation: one field for the summer crop,

DRESSED FROM HEAD TO TOE IN
MEDIEVAL GARB,
THIS VOLUNTEER FROM THE
MUSEUMSDORF DÜPPEL
WEAVES WOOL INTO CLOTH ON AN
ANCIENT MANUAL LOOM
THAT IS STILL BEING USED IN MANY
PARTS OF THE WORLD.
(PHOTO: MUSEUMSDORF DÜPPEL)

THE INTERIOR OF THIS RECONSTRUCTED
FARM DWELLING DEMONSTRATES
THE SPARTAN EXISTENCE THE GERMAN
PEASANTRY ENDURED FOR CENTURIES.
(PHOTO: MUSEUMSDORF DÜPPEL)

THE "SKUDDE" SHEEP ARE AN ENDANGERED SPECIES
FROM THE SOUTHERN BALTIC REGION, WHOSE ANCESTRY
CAN BE TRACED BACK TO THE STONE AGE.

one for the winter crop, and one that lay fallow. The Düppel Village Museum not only uses the same methods, but also manages to grow many plants from Medieval strains. "When the theater was bombed in Nuremberg, they discovered ancient seeds that had melted in a glass vessel which had been buried in the building's foundations," recalls Dr. Klaus Goldmann, one of the museum's directors. "A biologist from the University of Nuremberg analyzed the seeds and discovered they were from old genetic strains, some on the world's endangered species list. We planted these in our fields at Düppel."

The herb garden whose layout was inspired by a Swiss Medieval monastery, contains both rare and common plants including thyme, lavender, tarragon, marjoram, caraway seeds, dill, cucumbers, and red cabbage. The only controversial plant experiment turned out to be a strain of German hemp, once used for making linen cloth. When the local authorities learned that the plant (normally linked with marijuana) was growing in the garden, local newspapers dubbed the site the "Hash Museum."

"When the police understood that we were only growing the plant for scientific purposes, they said that we could continue to plant it, provided we put a locked cage around it, and let no one go near it," recalls Goldmann, unable to resist laughing. "With such constraints, it made more sense to remove the plant altogether."

As part of its endeavor to revive certain aspects of agriculture and animal domestication common to the Middle Ages, the museum has

succeeded in breeding an endangered species of sheep that goes back to the Stone Age in the Southern Baltic region. Known as "Skudde," the animal has long, stringy hair, similar to the nap in a Greek *flokati* rug. Shorn every spring by volunteers, its wool is then spun by hand and woven into cloth on a Medieval loom. This cloth will later be made into tunics and breeches for men and loose-fitting, ankle-length dresses and smocks for women—the chosen garb of the volunteers, which adds a singular touch of authenticity. While German visitors find such activities quaint, Turkish visitors often comment that wool is still spun and woven in this way in rural Turkey.

A free-range pig, which strongly resembles its wild-boar cousin, the "Düppeler Weideschwein," was bred back through genetic implementation of the root stock line. "We have seen such pigs in the drawings of Albrecht Dürer, so we know they existed in Germany," notes Goldmann.

The Düppel Village Museum enlightens visitors about Berlin's little-known Medieval history, all the while entertaining them with demonstrations of different rural crafts. By reviving this specific aspect of Germany's rich, albeit oftimes forgotten heritage, including various species of endangered plants and animals, it demonstrates that archaeology can not only permit us to retrace the past, but can actually help us to rediscover and preserve earth's bounty for generations to come.

The Film Museum-Potsdam

Schloss Strasse 1
14467 Potsdam
Tel: (0331) 271–8113

Open Tuesday through Friday
10:00 A.M. to 5:00 P.M.
Open Saturday, Sunday,
and holidays
10:00 A.M. to 6:00 P.M.

S-Bahn: 7 to Potsdam-Stadt
Tram: 92, 93, 96, 98
Bus: 601, 602, 603, 606

In-house cinema, café-restaurant.

IN a curious twist of fate, the Third Reich's most extravagant movie, Veit Harlan's *Kolberg*, which cost over eight million Reichsmarks (the equivalent of 40 million DM today) to produce, never did attract much of an audience. This epic motion picture, which dramatizes the 1807 victory of Kolberg (now Koxobrzeg, Poland), over the French army's siege, employed more extras (some of whom, in fact, were soldiers returning from the Eastern front) than the original number of combatants in the historic confrontation. Both Adolf Hitler and his propaganda

THE FILM MUSEUM IN POTSDAM IS LOCATED IN
THE HANDSOMELY RENOVATED ROYAL STABLES BUILT BY THE "SOLDIER KING"
FRIEDRICH WILHELM I,
AND LATER ENLARGED BY HIS SON, FREDERICK THE GREAT.

chief, Joseph Goebbels (who scripted the film's bombastic speeches), had hoped the movie would inspire the German citizenry to sacrifice their lives for the Reich.

Unfortunately for them, their timing was off. By the time *Kolberg* was released in January 1945, most cinemas in Germany had been destroyed. Even the print that had to be dropped by parachute into the German-held town of La Rochelle failed to have the requisite impact, since the Breton port was soon overrun by the surrounding Allied Armies. Most Germans born after World War II—apart from ardent film buffs—have never heard of *Kolberg,* and this is not altogether surprising, since, like other Nazi propaganda films, it cannot be commercially released. A visit to the Film Museum in Potsdam affords the opportunity to learn about its fascinating history in the exhibition dedicated to the Film City of Babelsberg—once the Hollywood of Continental Europe.

Located on two floors in the handsomely renovated former royal stables in Potsdam, built under the "Soldier King," and enlarged by his son Frederick the Great, the exhibition documents the history of Babelsberg's studios through a series of eight staged rooms designed by film directors, scenic designers, and film historians.

Although early production companies used the rooftops of Berlin as movie locations, by 1912 the Berlin cameraman and inventor, Guido Seeber, had moved his Bioscope Film Company to Babelsberg, where the grounds were spacious and uninhabited, and no one was disturbed whenever the highly flammable film material caught fire. Babelsberg's first movie star was the Danish actress Asta Nielsen, who played the lead in such popular hits as *Der Totentanz*

THE DEFA 70-REFLEX CAMERA, THE FIRST 70-MILLIMETER CAMERA PRODUCED IN THE FORMER EAST GERMANY IN 1964, WAS USED TO MAKE MOTION PICTURE EPICS. THE ONLY OTHER COUNTRIES THAT HAD COMPARABLE EQUIPMENT WERE THE UNITED STATES AND THE FORMER SOVIET UNION.

(The Dance of Death) in 1912 and *Engelein (Little Angels)* in 1913. Both motion pictures brought the screen actress early fame and excellent box office receipts—the films' earnings would be used to enlarge the studio's grounds. Over the next several decades, the Film City of Babelsberg would expand to 460,000 square meters, and employ between 2,000 and 3,000 people.

World War I was still raging when the studios were enlisted to champion the German state's military policy. Recognizing the cinema's influential power, General Erich Ludendorff (who was Chief of the Third German Army Command), urged the establishment of a movie company dedicated to promoting the war effort. Under the direction of

THIS EXHIBIT, TITLED
"WE ARE MARCHING BEHIND OUR WAVING
STANDARD," ILLUSTRATES
THE WAY MOVIES WERE USED AS
PROPAGANDA
TO PROMOTE THE NAZI CAUSE
AND INSTILL PATRIOTIC FERVOR DURING
WORLD WAR II.

German financier and press lord Alfred Hugenberg, a new national film production consortium was created in November 1917, the UFA (Universum Film Aktiengesellschaft), backed by the government, a few banks, and such major industrial groups as AEG and Henkel.

By the 1920s, the UFA could claim the continent's most modern production facilities, as well as a major string of movie theaters, twenty-five in Berlin alone, including the two biggest, the UFA-Palast and the UFA-Theater, which had 2,500 and 1,000 seats, respectively. During the early Weimar years, UFA alone was producing more movies than the rest of Europe: 646 in 1921, 472 in 1922, 347 in 1923. While the number of movies diminished after 1924, it was only because the company wanted to produce longer, and often costlier films.

To demonstrate the contrast between off-screen reality and movie-set glamour, three furnished dressing-rooms (one attributed to Marlene Dietrich), face several rows of vintage theater seats, from which visitors can view clips from popular German musicals and dramas, starring such stars as Lilian Harvey and Zarah Leander (the "German Greta Garbo").

Dietrich (1901–1992) made her triumphant debut in Babelsberg as the cabaret singer Lola-Lola in *The Blue Angel,* based on the 1905 novel *Professor Unrath* (Professor Garbage) by Heinrich Mann, the eldest brother of Nobel Prize–winning novelist Thomas Mann. The day of the movie's premiere, April 30, 1930, Dietrich set sail for the United States. Refusing Goebbels' generous terms to return to Germany in 1934, Dietrich went back to Berlin only after the war.

Under the direction of Erich Pommer (1923–26) and with the collaboration of major American production companies, the UFA produced such classics as Fritz Lang's *Die Niebelungen* (1923–24) and *Metropolis* (1925–26), whose costumes, movie clips, and assorted memorabilia are included in the exhibition. "*The Niebelungen* was made to demonstrate that all the old German legends and ideals of chivalry and bravery had not died in World War I," notes Guido Altendorf, manager of special exhibitions. "While Lang traveled all through Germany looking for suitable locations to shoot the movie, he ended up concluding that none of them looked sufficiently 'Germanic.' So he built all the movie's sets at Babelsberg, even the Rhine." This costly five-hour epic was one of Hitler's favorite films, prompting Goebbels to ask Lang to become the head of Germany's film industry. However, the Jewish-born Lang refused his offer, opting instead to emigrate.

While artistically innovative, Friedrich Wilhelm Murnau's *Faust* and Lang's *Metropolis* proved prohibitively expensive. Despite the film company's financial collaboration with the American-based Metro and Paramount studios, by 1927 the UFA was reporting a deficit of 60 million marks. Only the political clout of Alfred Hugenberg saved it from collapse. Convincing the government that the demise of UFA would be a tremendous cultural loss to the nation, he persuaded Germany's central bank to refinance the company. By 1929, UFA had returned to solvency by producing lucrative escapist musicals and comedies that emulated those being made in Hollywood.

After Hitler came to power, the

UFA soon became a highly effective tool for Nazi propaganda, producing such devious and infamous movies as Veit Harlan's anti-Semitic *Jud Süss* (1933). In a frenzy of overeager obedience, the studio bosses also issued a formal resolution dismissing all Jewish artists as of March 1933. This decision resulted in a mass exodus of talent, including the producer Erich Pommer, the actors Peter Lorre and Lilian Harvey, the writer/director Billy Wilder, and the film composer Hans Eisler. Those who were unable to flee to safety were often murdered in concentration camps, including the Jewish director and actor Kurt Gerron, who had appeared in *The Blue Angel*. (Although Gerron had fled to Holland, he was extradited by the Nazis who forced him to shoot a film intended for the Red Cross, glorifying conditions at the Theresienstadt concentration camp in Czechoslovakia. Gerron never did live to see the final reel, and the bogus documentary was completed by another director.)

But even under a Fascist dictatorship, some talent managed to flourish. In 1943, to celebrate its twenty-fifth anniversary, the UFA released a masterpiece, Josef von Baky's *The Fantastic Adventures of Baron von Munchhausen*, seen as Germany's *Wizard of Oz*. "Apart from the extraordinary special effects, this was the first film in which there was a widespread use of dissolves," notes Altendorf. The glowing reception accorded this movie spectacular, which cost 6.6 million Reichsmarks to produce, only served to heighten Babelsberg's output, despite the war. At the time of Germany's surrender on May 8, 1945, when most theaters and newspapers had already been shut down, fifty films were still in production.

In April 1945, the Soviet Red Army marched into the Film City. In 1948, the Soviet government licensed the East German film company DEFA (Deutsche Film AG) to make movies, provided that it contribute a percentage of the box-office receipts to the USSR, a ruling in effect until the early Fifties. In October 1952 DEFA became a state-owned firm, with the Babelsberg studios serving as the main producers of East Germany's feature-run and television movies. Working on studio grounds steeped in tradition, the German Democratic Republic (until the end of its existence as a sovereign state), made 550 films for television and approximately 700 feature films— 160 of which were for children. Its total workforce grew to encompass about 2,400 people.

The museum aims to show that, contrary to what one might suppose, the DEFA was an oasis of cultural resistance in the former GDR, producing such acclaimed films as Wolfgang Staudte's anti-fascist *The Murderers Are Among Us* and the anti-militarist *For the King of Prussia*, satirizing Frederick the Great. East German films also tackled problems regarding the suppression of individual freedom and self-expression, such as Konrad Wolf's *Solo Sunny* and Heiner Carow's *The Legend of Paul and Paula*.

Today, in a unified Germany, Potsdam's Film Museum faces the challenge of examining and clarifying Babelsberg's extraordinary history. The enlightening exhibition on the Film City of Babelsberg is one that serious film buffs and professionals will be studying and reflecting upon for decades to come.

THIS REPLICA OF LILIAN HARVEY'S DRESSING ROOM
SHOWS A CELEBRITY STILL OF THE POPULAR STAR POSING WITH WILLY FRITSCH,
WHO WOULD LATER BECOME A MEMBER OF THE NAZI PARTY.
THIS PETITE, FIVE-FOOT-TALL ACTRESS, ONCE CALLED THE "QUEEN OF MUSICAL COMEDY,"
COULD SING IN FRENCH, ENGLISH, GERMAN, AND HUNGARIAN.

MARLENE DIETRICH'S MONOGRAMMED
NAVY-BLUE DRESSING-GOWN AND SILK CLUTCH BAG
ARE POIGNANT REMINDERS OF
THE ACTRESS'S EARLY TIES WITH THE BABELSBERG
FILM STUDIOS.

THIS SUMPTUOUS COSTUME
WAS MADE FOR *THE NIEBELUNG*—
A MOVIE DIRECTED BY FRITZ LANG
THAT WAS BASED ON
AN OLD GERMAN LEGEND.
WHEN THE DIRECTOR FAILED TO FIND
LOCATIONS HE DEEMED
SUFFICIENTLY GERMANIC LOOKING,
HE HAD ALL THE SETS
CONSTRUCTED IN BABELSBERG
(INCLUDING A REPLICA OF THE RHINE).

Gründerzeitmuseum im Gusthaus Mahlsdorf
Founders' Museum and Manor House-Mahlsdorf

Hultschiner Damm 333
12623 Berlin
Tel: 5–67–83–29

Open Wednesday and Sunday
10:00 A.M. to 6:00 P.M.
Guided tours available by prior
appointment.

S-Bahn: 5 to Mahlsdorf

Tearoom on premises.

A T first glance, this residence seems to offer all the comforts of a solid, prosperous middle-class home toward the end of the last century. In the master bedroom there are heavy, carved wooden twin beds on wheels, with headboards in the shape of Neoclassical pediments. At the foot of each bed are freshly pressed antique cotton underclothes; on each wood and marble-topped nightstand, a lit candle in a brass candlestick casts a soft light on the room's vintage photographs and sentimental painting

THIS HANDSOME AND SPACIOUS
STONE MANOR HOUSE BUILT AROUND 1780
HAS BEEN PAINSTAKINGLY RESTORED
TO ITS FORMER GLORY.

of a mother embracing her two infant children. On the marble-topped washstand is the ubiquitous porcelain basin and bowl for washing up, and a matching toiletry set.

Downstairs in the basement kitchen, the scrubbed wooden table

LIVE DEMONSTRATIONS OF A PIANOLA, A MECHANICAL HARMONIUM THAT REPLICATES THE SOUNDS OF A DOMESTIC ORCHESTRA, AND AN ORCHESTRION (THE FORERUNNER OF THE JUKEBOX) ARE GIVEN IN THE MUSIC ROOM.

displays a panoply of cooking utensils: a hand-cranked coffee mill, a porcelain vegetable tureen, a ceramic flour shaker, a steel meat slicer, a wooden cutting board. On the cast-iron stove and on the coal box are assorted steam irons, which weigh as much as ten pounds each. The wooden pump that brought water from the well, the tin basins and washboards, the linen press, as well as the extensive assortments of wooden bowls and porcelain molds and serving dishes, demonstrate the wide variety of tools needed to make a German household run smoothly at a time when there was no electricity, no running water, and no central heating.

While these domestic arrangements may appear incongruous in the former Communist working-class suburb of Mahlsdorf, nothing strikes visitors as more surprising than the presence of an authentic old pub, the Muhlack-Ritze from the Scheunenviertel section of Berlin, with its oak bar and zinc-topped counter, its cast-iron potbelly stove, its carved ceramic beer keg, its round wooden tables and bentwood chairs, its old glass cases displaying cigarettes, lighters, and candy. To add to the overall authenticity, the walls are decorated with signs admonishing customers not to engage in improper behavior—hardly characteristic of a bar whose regular customers were pimps and prostitutes.

The Founders' Museum and Manor House in Mahlsdorf represents an instructive microcosm of Gründerzeit Germany, with its outward middle-class propriety and hidden squalor. Named after the great manipulators who "founded" huge enterprises on the basis of paper and little else, and who led Germans into often frenzied and ruinous speculation, the Gründerzeit era may be compared to America's Gilded Age.

Flush with capital after winning the Franco-Prussian War (the French paid the Germans an indemnity of five billion gold francs with interest) and a rapidly expanding economy, many Germans spent their money as ostentatiously as possible to demonstrate their new-found prosperity. The quick, easy money earned from speculation made it possible for small tradesmen to pop champagne corks, for farmers to invest in racehorses, and for merchants to build ornate houses and decorate them with overblown furniture and artwork. However, beneath this glittering façade, the period was marked by a slackening in public morals, an increase in public drunkenness, and a heightened incidence of prostitution and sex crimes.

It was this extravagant, lurid, colorful world that Lothar Beerfelde wished to recreate in the late Fifties when East Germany was in the throes of building a Socialist state. Although born in 1927, Beerfelde had a special attachment to the Germany that existed prior to the Great War, a universe he knew intimately from growing up in the solid, middle-class comfort of his great-uncle Josef Brauner, an engineer at Mercedes-Benz who had worked on some of the company's first cars. (Most historians now recognize two Germans, Karl Benz and Gottlieb Daimler, as the major pioneers of the gasoline engine automobile, and the fathers of the modern car. Although both men never met, their two companies merged in 1926 to manufacture Mercedes-Benz cars.)

"Lothar loved this type of heavy, dark wooden furniture, which looked expensive, although it was made industrially," notes Carolina Winkler, a docent who gives tours of the museum. "They represented security

OUTFITTED WITH FRESHLY PRESSED SHEETS
AND BLEACHED ANTIQUE UNDERCLOTHES, THESE TWIN OAK BEDS RE-CREATE
THE STOLID MIDDLE-CLASS COMFORT OF THE GRÜNDERZEIT ERA.

THE PARLOR WITH ITS VELVET-UPHOLSTERED,
MACHINE-MADE NEO-RENAISSANCE FURNITURE AND FRAMED FAMILY PORTRAITS
EVOKES A BYGONE WORLD OF FORMAL PROPRIETY.

and a sense of home to him, reminding him of the furniture within his great-uncle's house. In the Fifties, East Germans wanted to get rid of it—people felt that it wasn't modern. Much of what is in this house, he was able to acquire from salvage and junk heaps."

What Beerfelde lacked was a place in which to display his finds. His search for suitable quarters to house his collection was answered in 1958, when he learned of a spacious, abandoned stone manor house (c. 1780) in Mahlsdorf. Undeterred by the fact that the house was without windows or doors, and devoid of electricity and central heating, he moved in, and slowly began repairing the house, replacing its wooden doors, windows, and flooring with salvaged bits of masonry and wood taken from houses that were being torn down in East Berlin.

Similarly, when he learned that the Muhlack-Ritze, a well-known East Berlin pub, had been earmarked for the wrecking ball, he found a way to transfer the bar and its contents to the basement of his new Mahlsdorf home.

Endowed with skillful hands as well as a trained eye (Beerfelde had learned to repair many old mechanical instruments and automatons while working in East Berlin's Markisches Museum), he succeeded in restoring the dilapitated house to its former state. He was even able to recapture the era's popular melodies by repairing a fine collection of mechanical instruments, including a pianola (a mechanical piano that "played" music rolls), a mechanical harmonium (its wide range of sounds replicated a domestic orchestra), and an orchestrion, the forerunner of the jukebox (which was lovingly

THIS LAVISHLY DECORATED DINING ROOM WITH ITS TWIN NEO-BAROQUE MIRRORS
AND MATCHING SIDEBOARDS, AND NEO-GOTHIC DINING TABLE AND CHAIRS,
SHOWS THE GERMAN MIDDLE-CLASSES' AVIDITY FOR LUXURY.

reconditioned after having been abandoned in a barn for fifteen years).

Within a few years after his move to Mahlsdorf, Beerfelde opened his home on Sundays to the curious, who wanted a glimpse of the carefully salvaged vestiges from this all-but-forgotten era. It wasn't long before this maverick East German had also caught the attention of the Stasi (the Ministry of State Security), who asked him to pass on information regarding any American soldiers who might be visiting the East. "Although Beerfelde admits to working for the Stasi for four years, he wasn't very useful to them," notes Winkler. "He wasn't interested in politics. Still, the Stasi contact was useful because, for awhile, they placed the house under historic protection."

It is likely that the Stasi contact provided Beerfelde with another sort of shield. In accordance with his personal proclivities, he held underground meetings for Berlin's gay community every Sunday in his Mahlsdorf home, gatherings that soon gained the code name of the "Sunday Club." "Until the 1970s, homosexuality was not officially accepted in the GDR," says Winkler. "Although the Stasi knew about the 'Sunday Club' and its activities, they never interfered with the meetings."

What was suspect in the former GDR was owning a substantial private collection of antiques. "Gründerzeit was not the style of the Communist Party," notes Winkler. "Here was something that was outside the norms, and which represented bourgeois values, not socialist ones." In 1973, the former East German government demanded that Beerfelde pay 10,000 DM in back taxes on his collection, a substantial sum which he was clearly unable to pay. "That was when he decided to give his antiques away," recalls Winkler. "His attitude

THIS FORMER PUB WITH ITS OAK BAR AND ZINC-TOPPED COUNTER,
AND ITS SIGN *TANZEN VERBOTEN* (DANCING FORBIDDEN), WAS ONCE FREQUENTED BY
LADIES OF THE EVENING AND THEIR PROTECTORS.

was 'better the people should have it than the state.' This represented a very big sacrifice for him." It was only after Beerfelde's plight came to the attention of the influential East German lawyer Friedrich Karl Kaul (who was well-connected with the East German authorities and the gay community), that the tax suit was eventually dropped.

Yet, even after Germany's unification, Beerfelde's troubles were not over. Lulled into thinking that, with the fall of the Berlin Wall, a new liberalism had set in, he changed his name to Charlotta von Mahlsdorf, grew his hair long, and openly walked around in a housedress and apron, masquerading as a housekeeper from the Gründerzeit era. "People thought he was a bit eccentric, but not dangerous," says Winkler. "I think Beerfelde dressed this way because he saw himself as serving the objects in his home." In 1991, after Neo-Nazi "skinheads" crashed a party at his home, Beerfelde felt his security was threatened and began taking steps to emigrate. Since 1997, he has been residing in Sweden, presiding over a similar museum with those pieces in his collection he refused to leave behind. (The remainder was sold to the City of Berlin for 500,000 DM.)

Today, the Founders' Museum and Manor House offers visitors private tours (its highlight remains the demonstration of different mechanical instruments), chamber music concerts, and piano recitals with local artists, as well as literary soirées presenting different East and West German writers. What began as one man's quest to preserve a piece of Germany's past has spurred other volunteers to create a haven for intellectual and cultural enrichment, one where visitors can also better appreciate the attractions and foibles of the Gründerzeit era.

Grunewald Hunting Lodge

Am Grunewaldsee
14193 Berlin-Zehlendorf
Tel: 813–35–97

Open Tuesday through Sunday
10:00 A.M. to 1:00 P.M. and
1:30 P.M. to 5:00 P.M.
April to October

Bus: 115, 183

It is quite likely that, had the citizens of Berlin and Cölln not joined together in 1539 with an urgent petition requesting that Joachim II Hector, Elector of Brandenburg, make all their churches Lutheran, the Hohenzollern ruler would not have been able to raise the funds to build his handsome hunting lodge in the Grunewald. Not only did the German prince agree to convert to Lutheranism himself, he also used the occasion to justify his seizure of all church lands and assets, as well as the property belonging to those Jews who were summarily expelled from the city. With this newly found wealth at his disposal, Joachim commissioned Caspar Theyss (who also rebuilt Berlin's former Stadtschloss) to

AFTER SEIZING ALL THE CHURCH'S LANDS AND ASSETS,
JOACHIM II HECTOR, THE ELECTOR OF BRANDENBURG,
WAS ABLE TO FINANCE THE BUILDING OF THIS HANDSOME FORTIFIED CASTLE.

design a handsome fortified castle in 1542 on the eastern side of the Havel lake amid the dense pines of the Grunewald forest.

Over the entrance door visitors can still see the carved inscription, *Zum Grünen Wald* (To the Green Wood), from which the lodge took its name. (Because the road from the city to the Grunewald passed over treacherous marshy ground, Joachim ordered that a long causeway of logs—a Damm—be constructed. In time, this Damm became known to all Berliners as the Kurfürstendamm, "the road of the Prince Electors.")

When the lodge was originally built, it was surrounded by a wide moat, and a wooden drawbridge led to the gateway entrance. Today, the whitewashed, red-tile-roofed edifice stands in a gravel-covered courtyard, surrounded by various later additions, including a weapons arsenal built by Frederick the Great, which now serves as a museum of hunting equipment. (Prior to its opening in 1975, this historic museum had to obtain a license from the U.S. Army, because its collection included an extensive display of guns made between the sixteenth and the nineteenth century.) In 1693, after Frederick III, the Prince of Oranienburg, came to power, he commissioned Arnold Nering to transform the lodge into a Baroque dwelling. Most of the windows on the ground floor and second floor were enlarged, the sandstone framework was removed, and the moat was filled in.

Little remains of the original Renaissance architecture, apart from the windows in the lodge's tower, the spiral staircase, and the relief depicting two rutting stags over the entrance above the inscription describing the laying of the building's foundation stone on March 7, 1542. In the imposing Great Hall, one can admire a painted coffered Renaissance ceiling, discovered beneath Baroque stuccowork.

One of the few Renaissance edifices remaining in Berlin, the Grunewald Hunting Lodge boasts a surprisingly fine collection of paintings from the Northern School, including work by such Old Masters as Lucas Cranach the Elder and Lucas Cranach the Younger, Jan Steen, Jacob Jordaens, Willem Cornelisz Duyster, Jan Lievens, and Ferdinand Bol (Rembrandt's most accomplished pupil). Its charming, rustically furnished rooms also reveal the Hohenzollern princes' long-standing passion for collecting

NEXT TO THIS SATIN-COVERED BAROQUE CHAIR IS A STILL-LIFE (C.1670) OF AN ORACH PLANT SURROUNDED BY TOADSTOOLS, SNAKES, AND BUTTERFLIES BY THE DUTCH PAINTER OTTO MARSEUS VAN SCHRIECK.

THIS PAINTED WOODEN MERMAID WITH TWO TAILS ENSCONCED IN THIS WROUGHT-IRON CHANDELIER WAS MADE IN SOUTHERN GERMANY AROUND 1700.

antiques and works of art associated with the hunt.

Hunting was the exclusive right of the sovereign and the right to game was sacrosanct. Woe to the peasant rash enough to capture the hare eating any cabbages in his garden. A regiment of gamekeepers was ever alert to prosecute any such crime of *lèse-majesté*.

Born in Berlin, Joachim II (1505–1571) was not only an enthusiastic soldier and huntsman, but an amateur of both the arts and sciences, as well. His passion for hunting was so pronounced that in addition to this lodge, he also built hunting lodges in Potsdam, Köpenick, Rüdersdorf, Schönebeck, Zossen, Grimnitz, Letzlingen, and Küstrin. While the Grunewald Hunting Lodge was used for the next four hundred years by the Hohenzollern dynasty, it wasn't always used for hunting. "Frederick the Great hated hunting with a passion," notes Prof. Dr. Winfried

Baer, the curator of Schloss Charlottenburg. "He was the first Prussian king who never hunted."

Almost a century would pass before Prince Charles of Prussia, one of the sons of Friedrich Wilhelm III, revived the first mounted hunt since 1740, and made it an annual event on November 3, St. Hubert's Day or *Hubertustag*. (Legend has it that Hubert, patron saint and protector of the hunt, saw the cross of Jesus surrounded by a glorious halo suspended between golden reindeer antlers, while hunting on a Sunday. The vision was sufficient to compel Hubert to give up hunting and become a devout Christian, two acts which earned him sainthood in 772.)

No Hohenzollern ruler was more passionate about hunting than Kaiser Wilhelm II. To compensate for a birth defect that resulted in a slightly shorter left arm, the Kaiser trained himself to be a crack shot, and photos show that he was able to

THE GREAT HALL FEATURES A STRIKING PAINTED COFFERED RENAISSANCE CEILING
AND PAINTINGS BY LUCAS CRANACH THE ELDER, AND HIS SON.

shoot using only his good arm. He also was a skilled swordsman and spear thrower. The Hohenzollern's 1908 yearbook shows the German Emperor posing proudly before his numerous trophies. According to carefully kept court records, he single-handedly killed 61,694 individual game within a span of twenty years! Little wonder then, that the cumulative effect of so much grapeshot left him deaf in one ear.

Although Wilhelm II made a number of domestic improvements to the lodge, by 1907 he had stopped going to Grunewald, preferring instead to frequent a forest where he would not be disturbed by other unwelcome visitors from Berlin. To make sure he had sufficient game to hunt, he ordered hundreds of animals to be captured in Grunewald, and transferred to the forest of Schorfheide, the largest expanse of woods in the imperial family's possession.

After World War I, with the fall of the German Empire, the lodge became a city museum presenting some of the paintings collected over the centuries by the Hohenzollern's Brandenburg branch. Paintings by the two Cranachs and their school demonstrate the artistic preferences of Joachim I and his successor. The lodge possesses one of the finest works by Lucas Cranach the Younger, a life-size portrait of Joachim II (c. 1555), emphasizing the sitter's grandiloquent appearance and sumptuous court dress.

There are also several scenes from the Passion, produced in the workshop of Lucas Cranach the Elder, originally made for the now-destroyed church of the Dominican convent on Berlin's palace square. Among the nine oil paintings on wood that have been preserved are the *Washing of Christ's Feet, Christ on the Mount of Olives, Ecce Homo, The Scourging of Christ, The Carrying of the Cross,*

THIS UPSTAIRS HALL BOASTS TWO PAINTINGS BY JACOB JORDAENS,
THE OLD PEOPLE SING, THE YOUNG PEOPLE PLAY (C. 1645)
AND THE SIGNED *SUSANNA AND THE TWO OLD MEN* (1657),
A MORALITY TALE ABOUT TWO LASCIVIOUS MEN WHO ARE MORTALLY PUNISHED
AFTER FALSELY ACCUSING THE VIRTUOUS YOUNG WOMAN OF ADULTERY.

The Burial, and *The Resurrection*.

While the collection contains many hunting scenes (every Hohenzollern prince had his stable of hunt painters), as well as a number of fine works by Anton Graff (regarded as the most important eighteenth-century German portrait painter), an outstanding group of Dutch paintings, acquired by the Great Elector and his successors, remains the museum's principal attraction.

Not to be missed is Jacob Jordaens' genre scene *The Old People Sing, The Young People Play* (c. 1645), an allegorical work portraying a family banquet, that contrasts the enjoyment of life with its transience, exemplified by the skull and the painting's inscription, *cognita mori* (think on death). Ferdinand Bol's impressive *Portrait of a Young Man* (signed *F.*

Bol fec 1643), follows the example of his teacher, Rembrandt, in both the subject's posture and clothing, as well as in the use of light and dark. Jan Steen's *Women Smoking* (c. 1675) hints at the mutability and fragility of life, with its smoking motif and its depiction of an elderly widow seated with a younger woman in her prime.

Visiting the handsomely restored Jagdschloss Grunewald today, it is hard to imagine that the lodge was taken over and vandalized by unruly mobs of soldiers after Germany's surrender during the last war. Many of the paintings were thrown through the windows into the courtyard and left out in the open for days. Some were even used as targets by riflemen, who, in one instance, tried to shoot out the eyes in the portrait of a Prussian princess. Moreover, in 1945,

IOACHIMVS DEI GRA
TIA MARCHIO BRAN
DENBVRGENSIS ÆTATIS
EI VS SE DE CIMO ANNO
VERO SA LV TIS 15 2 0

THIS PORTRAIT ON WOOD OF JOACHIM PRINCE OF ANHALT (1504–1551),
PAINTED BY LUCAS CRANACH THE ELDER AROUND 1521,
IS NOTABLE FOR ITS METICULOUSLY DETAILED ARMOR AND FINERY.
(PHOTO: STIFTUNG PREUSSISCHE SCHLÖSSER UND GÄRTEN BERLIN-BRANDENBURG,
SCHLOSS CHARLOTTENBURG, FOTOTHEK)

most of the Grunewald's trees were cut down to provide Berlin with desperately needed fuel.

Subsequent replanting has now restored the forest to its original character, complete with stocks of red and fallow deer, wild boar, and mouflon. Today the luxuriant forest is filled with families and frolicking dogs on weekends, who often seem oblivious to the riches contained inside the whitewashed Renaissance lodge.

Knowing that the Grunewald Hunting Lodge was the first museum to reopen after the war, in May 1949—less than a year after the Soviet-backed Berlin Blockade nearly brought the city to its knees—one cannot help but admire the determination and passionate commitment of Berlin's museum specialists and restorers. Thanks to their dedicated initiative, a fine collection of Northern masters was saved from utter ruin and an elegant museum was preserved as a tribute to the rich heritage of the Hohenzollern dynasty in Germany.

**Sophie-Gips-Höfe Berlin
Sophienstrasse 21
10178 Berlin
Tel: 284–991–21**

**Open Saturday
11:00 A.M. to 5:00 P.M.
Visits by appointment only.**

U-Bahn: 8 to Weinmeisterstrasse

B RIGHTLY colored oversize typeface art by Lawrence Weiner decorates the side of a renovated industrial building and a massive curved and rusted tungsten-steel sculpture by Richard Serra greets visitors at the entrance. There are oversize, haunting color-photograph portraits by Nan Goldin and Thomas Ruff that have exposed sitters to an unforgiving, penetrating lens and a conceptual installation by Felix Gonzalez Torres consisting of a closet-like space filled with a mountain of gold-cellophane-wrapped sucking candy, samples of which every visitor is welcome to take. In another space, there is a see-through glass dining-room table shaped like a painter's palette, and supported by a female mannequin on all fours, dressed seductively in a green diving-suit and matching green high-heel lace-up boots. A peephole in the floor allows visitors to see and hear Pipilotti Rist's mesmerizing video representing a "window into the earth," titled *Selfless in the Lava Bath*, depicting a nude woman emerging from a cave, and asking to be rescued in many different languages.

Welcome to the Hoffmann Collection, a selection of works chiefly by American and European artists that were made primarily during the 1970s and 1980s. Located in the heart of the former Jewish quarter in East Berlin, this unusual gallery is the culmination of an ambitious dream by two business and culture mavericks, Erika and Rolf Hoffmann. Presented over two floors, in a space spanning 1,800 square meters, the collection is displayed in

a renovated factory, which was converted into a public gallery and private living quarters.

"This factory building was built between 1890 and 1905, and was first used for manufacturing sewing machines, and more recently medical instruments in the former GDR," notes the petite, elegant Erika Hoffmann. "When it was clear that it would no longer be used for industrial purposes, we acquired it from the Treuhand, the organization set up to restructure East Germany's industry after unification. We came here four years ago, when the district was virtually deserted, apart from tenants who had been living here for years in low-rent apartments, most without even telephones. People thought we were crazy, they didn't understand why we were doing this.

"But we wanted the East German people, in particular, to be able to come here and discover the kind of art which—for so long—had been banned in their country. We wanted to do something positive for the area."

To the Hoffmanns, the fall of the Berlin Wall in 1989 represented not only a political watershed but also a crucial cultural and historical breakthrough: Europe would soon again be a cultural entity reaching to the Ural Mountains, and the reunited Germany would eventually be in a position to expand beyond its bipolar East versus West syndrome. Moving from Cologne to Berlin with their collection was an opportunity for them to experience firsthand the struggle for a new cultural equilibrium between East and West, and to take part in the formation of Germany's new cultural identity, which they would both confront and to which they would both contribute.

Instead of making financial demands on the new German capital—whose cultural budget had already been stretched perilously thin—they came up with a plan that would permit them to finance and maintain a spacious and innovative gallery space, hire a curatorial staff, and even create a rent-free studio for an artist-in-residence program. Their jealously guarded independence is understandable given the three frustrating years they spent negotiating with the city of Dresden to build a stunning contemporary art museum at their own expense which was to be designed by their friend Frank Stella. (All that remains of this project is a scale model of the proposed museum, along with an elegant promotional catalogue.)

The beginnings of this collection go back to the early Seventies, when Erika and Rolf Hoffmann were building a successful fashion company. The encounters and personal relationships that they had with such artists as Andy Warhol, Jean-Michel Basquiat, and Felix Gonzalez-Torres not only fueled their work as designers, but extended their understanding of art and its infinite possibilities. Having sold their company in the late Eighties, they were not only able to concentrate even more on their passion to collect, but also to pursue the diverse directions that contemporary art was taking, particularly in such Seventies' conceptual art movements as ZERO and Arte Povera. It is this striking and often compelling diversity of artistic expression that they wish to share with the city of Berlin.

Choosing one of the oldest parts of Berlin—the Spandauer Vorstadt—

THE WORKS IN THIS VAST SPACE
RAISE QUESTIONS ABOUT ENTRANCES AND OBSTRUCTIONS,
WHETHER IT'S THE LARGE FELT SCULPTURE BY ROBERT MORRIS,
THE FUR-COVERED CHAIR,
OR THE WOODEN CRATE SCULPTURE BY RICHARD ARTSCHRAGER.

they and their children undertook the ambitious renovation and restoration of a rundown factory and residential complex (renamed the Sophie-Gips-Höfe) for which they and their architects Becker, Gewers, Kühn & Kühn created a new passageway open to the public during the day between Sophienstrasse and Gipsstrasse. Included in the renovation were three old city houses on Sophienstrasse and a remodeling of the former factory floors into loft apartments and galleries, as well as offices for an architectural firm, a radio station, and a delicatessen-café. Working within the microcosm of the Sophie-Gips-Höfe, the Hoffman's intention is to open up their collection in a context that shows visitors the natural correlation between business and culture. The mix reflects the couple's conviction that the most vital art emerges from a nexus of public and private concerns, aesthetics and business, work and play.

Yet, as has been true in other city neighborhoods, such as in New York's Soho district, the blend of art and commerce has engendered certain misgivings. "It's true that since the Hoffmanns moved here more galleries and exclusive shops have opened up," notes the collection's curator Sabrina Van der Ley. "There is now a contrast of rich and poor, and some gallery owners and Leftist intellectuals complain that the neighborhood is becoming too expensive. They are worried that, with the delicatessens and cafés around here, this area is going to become the next Soho."

Nonetheless, even with such caveats, the newly renovated outdoor courtyards and the interior gallery space have proven to be a successful blend of the new and the old, the rough and the elegant. Almost every inch of the new complex is an attempt to blend the practical with the aesthetic. Punctuating the renovated buildings and courtyard gardens are works by four conceptual artists: Gunda Förster's lit spaces in the passageway, Thomas Locher's vertical wall-covering word piece in the first courtyard, Teresa Murak's lawn sculpture, and Lawrence Weiner's poetic sentence, which has been strung high up on the wall facing the complex's garden.

Wherever feasible, the industrial materials and original design of the buildings have been retained, although freshened with paint, new wood flooring, and state-of-the-art lighting. Yet, because the Hoffman's furniture and fresh flowers in corrugated tin buckets are interspersed throughout the space (many visitors are surprised to see a stunning, double-bed made of carved oak), the overall effect is one of both intimacy and informality—a notable departure from other galleries and collections in Germany. "To have a private collection presented this way is very new in Germany," notes Van der Ley. "It is very un-German to blend public space with private space. You don't have strangers coming into your house just to see how you live. This is something that isn't normally done."

The collection reveals a fascination with a variety of unusual and avant-garde artistic trends, ranging from such contemporary icons as Andy Warhol and Tom Wesselman's Pop Art, to Dan Flavin's light sculptures, Donald Judd's steel wall cubes, to the lesser-known kinetic, mechanistic art of artists such as Gianni Colombo, Jean Tinguely, Günther Vecker, and Heinz Mack, who have often been regrouped in the ZERO art movement. The works on display show that almost anything may have the potential of being material for art, be it a circular mound of gravel and wire by

Reiner Ruthenbeck (a pupil of the conceptual artist Josef Beuys), three color-photo portraits by Rineke Dijkstra of naked women who have just given birth, dazedly holding their new-born infants, as well as an elegant wall made exclusively of superimposed rusted aluminum tins filled with old papers, by Christian Boltanski, appropriately titled *The Archives of C.B.*

"This collection is very challenging to the visitor, and even to me, at times," admits Van der Ley. "These pieces question one's notion of beauty. You can either hate a piece or love it. There is rarely any middle ground. Perhaps the idea behind some of these works is to wake us up, to stop us in our tracks. I also think they're about the strangeness of the imagination." One thing is certain— whether one is a newcomer to the contemporary art world or a seasoned gallerygoer, it is difficult to dispute the notion that the Hoffmann collection remains unique, not just for what it contains, but also for its thought-provoking intentions.

THIS CONFERENCE ROOM
WITH ITS ROUGH CORRUGATED-IRON CEILING
AND ELEGANT BRUSHED-STEEL TABLE
FEATURES AN EXCEPTIONAL COLLECTION OF EARLY ABSTRACT
AND CONSTRUCTIVIST PAINTINGS,
INCLUDING WORKS BY
DUNCAN GRANT, VANESSA BELL, JEAN ARP,
AND ALEXANDER RODCHENKO.

A CHARCOAL DRAWING OF "BLACK ANNA" FOR THE SEGMENT
TITLED *OUTBREAK* IS PART OF THE TRENCHANT SERIES
ON THE GERMAN PEASANTS' WAR.
THE ORIGINAL BELONGS TO
THE COLLECTION OF THE KUNSTHALLE BREMEN.
(PHOTO: KÄTHE KOLLWITZ MUSEUM)

Käthe Kollwitz Museum

Fasanenstrasse 24
10719 Berlin
Tel: 882-52-10

Open Wednesday through Monday
11:00 A.M. to 6:00 P.M.

U-Bahn: 1 to Kurfürstenstrasse
Bus: 109, 119, 129, 219, 249

Knowing, as we do, that the poor and the oppressed were her primary source of inspiration, it seems a curious paradox that the museum devoted to Germany's most important twentieth-century female graphic artist and sculptor, Käthe Kollwitz (1867–1945), is located on a fashionable street off the Kurfürstendamm. Housed in a private mansion built in 1871, this elegant museum seems a thousand miles away from Prenzlauerberg, Berlin's heavily populated working-class district, where Kollwitz worked and lived for fifty years. It was there that the artist produced her outstanding body of graphic art, notably in the field of self-portraiture, which has induced art historians to call her the "female Rembrandt."

After being largely destroyed by bombing during World War II, this handsome Neoclassical building was painstakingly restored by the City of Berlin and the Deutsche Bank, and topped with a skylit dome during the 1980s. The four-story museum inside was established in 1986 by the art dealer, collector, and artist Hans Pels-Leusden who donated to it his collection of one hundred prints, seventy drawings and posters, and

THE FOUR-STORY KÄTHE KOLLWITZ MUSEUM
IS A HANDSOME NEOCLASSICAL BUILDING WHICH,
AFTER BEING LARGELY DESTROYED
BY WORLD WAR II BOMBING,
WAS BEAUTIFULLY RESTORED IN THE 1980s.

PHOTOGRAPHS OF KÄTHE KOLLWITZ ALONE AND WITH HER HUSBAND, THE PHYSICIAN DR. KARL KOLLWITZ, DOMINATE THE FIRST-FLOOR GALLERY.

fifteen sculptures. Not only is this collection notable for its comprehensiveness, presenting the artist's oeuvre from 1888 through 1942, it also contains some of her finest drawings and graphic work, including the series of *Self-Portraits,* the woodcuts relating to the *Peasants' Rebellion* (1902–1906) and *War* (1922–23), as well as such important sculptures as *The Lamentation* (1938) dedicated to the Expressionist sculptor, Ernst Barlach.

Born in Königsberg, East Prussia, Kollwitz was encouraged by her father to study art, both in Berlin and in Munich. In 1904, she traveled to Paris, where she met Auguste Rodin and Théophile-Alexandre Steinlen, the satirical Swiss graphic artist, both of whom were to have a substantial impact on her work. However, it was the artist and etcher Max Klinger who would help her to crystalize her inclination toward graphic art. In his pamphlet, *Painting and Drawing,* Klinger maintained that some themes should be *drawn* rather than painted; the graphic arts, he asserted, could better express the darker aspects of life. They had their own role to play, their own validity, and were entitled to the same consideration as painting. Reading this, Kollwitz felt she had discovered her true calling as an artist. Henceforth, she would devote her life to art forms in which color was absent, or at best, subordinate: drawing, graphics, and sculpture.

As the wife of the physician Dr. Karl Kollwitz, the artist witnessed first-hand the poverty, disease, and deprivation that afflicted the population of Prenslauerberg. The eloquent lines and stark contrasts between light and dark in her drawings underscore the miserable living and working conditions that countless women, men, and children were forced to endure.

While the harsh beauty in these works makes them memorable, their subject matter challenged and troubled the German Kaiser and his family. Kollwitz's 1906 poster depicting seamstresses toiling late into the night so disturbed the German Empress that she refused to open an exhibition devoted to *Deutsch Heimarbeit* (the German cottage industry) as long as this poster was used to publicize it. Undaunted by this rejection, in 1924 the artist produced the poster *Brot (Bread)* for the International Workers Union as part of a portfolio of prints titled *Hunger*. It shows a despairing mother, unable to provide for her children, hiding her face in shame, while one famished child tugs at her skirt and another cries bitterly.

The 1903 premiere of Gerhard Hauptmann's play *The Weavers,* which dramatized the desperate uprising and defeat of the Silesian weavers in 1844, proved to be a milestone for Kollwitz's work, as she later wrote in her diary. It was to inspire one of her most powerful series of lithographs, entitled *Weavers Uprising,* produced between 1893 and 1897. The series caused a sensation, for it was one of the first times that such powerful drawings had portrayed the workers' struggle sympathetically. Displayed at the Berlin Art Exhibition in 1898, the show's jury, which was composed of established artists, nominated this group of drawings for a gold medal. Fearing the possible social repercussions if such an honor were bestowed on this work, Kaiser Wilhelm II called the series of lithographs "gutter art," and vetoed the award.

Confronted daily by the misery in her own district, it was inevitable that the passionate and sensitive Kollwitz would identify and side with its principal victims. In her series of lithographs *The Peasants' Rebellion*

THE SCULPTURE *WAVING WOMEN* DEPICTS A GROUP OF WOMEN BIDDING GOOD-BYE TO THEIR SONS AS THEY GO OFF TO WAR.

(based on the peasants' revolt against their exploitation by the nobility and the church in the early sixteenth century), the artist portrayed herself as "Black Anna" leading a ragged and angry mob. "By returning to an event that took place 400 years earlier, Kollwitz expresses her solidarity with the underclass, particularly women of her own day," explains Dr. Gudrun Fritsch, one of the museum's founding members and its chief docent.

Yet, in her autobiographical *Retrospective on Earlier Times,* Kollwitz explains how her depiction of the working classes was initially motivated by aesthetic considerations. "For me, beauty was the Königsberger porter, beauty was the Polish Jimkies on their cargo ships, beauty was the grandeur of the people and the grace of their movements. The bourgeoisie had no appeal for me, whereas the workers affected me deeply. Not until much later did I fully comprehend

the fate of the workers and all the resulting repercussions."

The museum's collection also shows how the relationship between mother and child was central to the artist's work. Not only did Kollwitz believe that motherhood was an important experience in a woman's life, bringing her genuine happiness, she was also preoccupied by the thoughts of death separating mother from child, as in the print *Woman with Dead Child* (1903). This print, showing an anguished mother clutching her dead child, in which the artist and her son Peter served as models, is hauntingly prophetic. Peter would be killed in Flanders, Belgium, shortly after the outbreak of World War I.

While her son's tragic death would cast a shadow over the rest of Kollwitz's life, it would also inspire some of her most compelling graphic art and sculpture, including the renowned *Mother with Dead Son* (1937–38), which many have likened to a modern-day Pietà. Today, a monumental bronze cast of this moving work dominates the impressively empty space inside Schinkel's *Neue Wache* (Guard House), Germany's official war memorial dedicated to the victims of war and tyranny on the Unter den Linden. Nonetheless, even as Kollwitz was able to demonstrate consummate artistry in works fueled by the theme of war, she never ceased to wrestle with the motivations that led to so much bloodshed: "Who are the guilty ones?" she queried in her diary. "Do they exist, or has everybody been betrayed? Doesn't youth have any judgement? Do the young ones obey so easily without thinking? Do they actually want war?"

This questioning self is eternally etched in her series of *Self-Portraits*, which she began in her early twenties. While most of these portrayals are characterized by melancholy and a quiet desperation, they also reveal an uncommon dignity and self-assertion. Focusing mainly on her facial expression, the artist strives to plumb the depths of her personality, divesting herself of any prettifying details. Her self-portraits reveal the heavy toll of sorrow and disappointment upon her spirit, culminating with her dismissal as Head of the Master Class for Graphic Arts at the Prussian Academy of Art and the banning of her work after Hitler's rise to power.

In one lithograph produced in 1934, when she was sixty-seven years old, Kollwitz shows through her set jaw and tense forehead, her inability to protest verbally or even artistically at that time. It was during this period that she confided to her diary: "During the past forty years, I have had the extreme good fortune of being able to exhibit my work. I have always provoked a response. Yet, I

THIS EARLY SELF-PORTRAIT OF KOLLWITZ AS A SMILING ART STUDENT
(A PENCIL-AND-BRUSH DRAWING IN BLACK INK) IS ONE OF THE COLLECTION'S HIGHLIGHTS.
(PHOTO: KÄTHE KOLLWITZ MUSEUM)

still find it hard to come to terms with the fact that I have lost this privilege, but I shall have to learn this and I will do so. I will remain loyal to the deprived people of this world."

Kollwitz completed her final work, a clay model for *Women Waiting for Men to Come Back from War*, in 1942. A year later, after her home was destroyed (together with a large body of her graphic work), she was forced to evacuate to Nordhausen. For the brief remainder of her life, she would stay on in Moritzburg, near Dresden, at the invitation of the Saxon Prince Ernst Heinrich. She died on April 25, 1945, two weeks before Germany's surrender.

Perhaps more than any other artist of this century, Käthe Kollwitz gave impressive, tangible form to the anguish of the downtrodden and the forgotten, working with tireless passion and a sense of mission. "I want my art to serve a purpose," she wrote in her diary in 1922. "I want it to have an impact in this day and age, when people are so desperate and in need of help." After viewing this impressive collection, one can only hope that the beauty and inexhaustible expressiveness of Käthe Kollwitz's work will continue to make its indelible mark on the world.

Kleinglienicke Castle

Königstrasse 36
14109 Berlin
Tel: 805–3041

**Open Saturday and Sunday
10:00 A.M. to 5:00 P.M.
Mid-May to Mid-October**

**S-Bahn: 1 to Wannsee, then take
Bus 116 to Konigstrasse**

**Garden restaurant open during
the summer season; seasonal
concerts offered in the Orangerie.**

AT the end of Berliner Strasse lies
the notorious wrought-iron Glienicke
Bridge built between 1905 and 1907,
an apt symbol for the Iron Curtain
that once divided East and West. It
was on "this bridge of spies," that the
American U-2 surveillance pilot Gary
Powers was traded for a Soviet agent,
and that the Jewish dissident Anatoly
Scharansky was permitted to cross
over into the West as an early gesture
of Gorbachev's *glasnost*. Today, this
very same bridge, reopened to normal
traffic since 1990, is a gateway to one
of the most enchanting estates on the
cityline of Potsdam, the Kleinglienicke
Castle and Park, a masterpiece of
Neoclassical architecture and English-

THE ENTRANCE TO KLEINGLIENICKE CASTLE AND PARK
DEMONSTRATES BOTH THE GENIUS OF SCHINKEL,
WHO CHANGED THE HUNTING LODGE INTO A QUASI-ROMAN VILLA,
AND THE INSPIRED TOUCH OF LENNÉ,
WHO TRANSFORMED THE PARK INTO AN IDYLLIC SETTING.

inspired landscape design.

Once an ornamental farm estate owned by Count Lindenau, who later sold it (in 1814), the rural property was utterly transformed after its acquisition by Prince Karl of Prussia in 1824. Because this high-born Hohenzollern (the brother of Friedrich Wilhelm III) had traveled extensively in Italy and was enamored with the Ancient World, he commissioned the architect Karl Friedrich Schinkel to convert the existing manor house into a summer palace modeled after a Roman villa, and to design a number of auxiliary structures for the vast grounds. Peter Josef Lenné (1789–1866), whose forbears were royal gardeners from Bonn, was entrusted with the landscaping of the 287-acre park, transforming the estate's northern end into a shaded, alpine terrain, and the southern end into a vista reminiscent of the prince's cherished Italy.

Here, away from the impersonal steel and glass buildings of downtown Berlin, visitors are struck by Lenné's successful collaboration with Schinkel, which harmoniously relates the buildings at Kleinglienicke ("Little Glienicke") with the park's winding paths, moss-covered shade trees, basket-shaped flower beds, and bronze and stone statuary of Greek and Roman gods and goddesses. Lenné is regarded as Prussia's greatest landscape architect, and in view of his extensive work for Prince Karl, it is not surprising that the museum at Kleinglienicke pays tribute to his accomplishments as both landscape designer and urban planner. Among the items on display are a handsome portrait, painted when Lenné was in his prime, and a gilded bronze laurel wreath awarded to the landscaper posthumously.

VISITORS TO THE ESTATE ARE STILL ENTHRALLED BY SCHINKEL'S CASINO OVERLOOKING THE HAVEL RIVER: A TWO-STORY ITALIANATE EDIFICE DECORATED WITH POMPEIAN FRESCOES, WHICH IS SET OFF BY GRACEFUL PERGOLAS AND COLUMNED TERRACES. (PHOTO: STIFTUNG PREUSSISCHE SCHLÖSSER UND GÄRTEN BERLIN-BRANDENBURG, SCHLOSS CHARLOTTENBURG, PHOTOTHEK)

IN KEEPING WITH THE STRUCTURE OF A ROMAN VILLA, THE ORIGINAL MANOR HOUSE
WAS REORIENTED AROUND AN OUTDOOR INTERIOR COURTYARD;
A COVERED TRELLIS WAS USED TO BRIDGE THE GAP BETWEEN THE HOUSE AND THE
STABLES, THUS HEIGHTENING THE FEELING OF ENCLOSURE AND PRIVACY.
(PHOTO: STIFTUNG PREUSSISCHE SCHLÖSSER UND GÄRTEN BERLIN-BRANDENBURG,
SCHLOSS CHARLOTTENBURG, PHOTOTHEK)

"Lenné was the most prolific land-scape designer, creating 360 gardens in Germany," notes Michael Seiler, Potsdam's Palaces garden director. "Although many of his designs burned during the war, we were lucky to discover the most complete plans of the grounds, which permitted us to restore the gardens to their former beauty."

Dubbed "the master of the panorama," Lenné significantly altered the appearance of Berlin and Potsdam during the first half of the nineteenth century, embellishing the banks of the Havel River by adding new walks and plantings, as well as linking gardens to the surrounding fields and streams. Through his inspired landscape design, he was able to create a unified view that brought together the parks of the Neuer Garten, Babelsberg, Sacrow, Pfaueninsel, and Kleinglienicke.

While the gilded griffons at the entrance to the estate and the magnificent Lion Fountain in front of the Italianate villa (a replica of a fountain at Rome's Villa Medici) were clearly intended to impress visitors with the stature of the Hohenzollern dynasty, the grounds and princely residence convey a sense of elegant simplicity and intimacy.

Although Schinkel made few changes to the interior layout of the two-story manor house, he reoriented the building around an outdoor interior courtyard, joining it to a covered trellis spanning the gap between the house and the stable block to enhance the feeling of enclosure—a novel design for the period.

It is a pity that the heir to Kleinglienicke, Prince Friedrich Leopold, was forced to sell most of his great-grandfather's collections in 1939, prior to emigrating to Austria. Nonetheless, the Schinkel-furnished rooms still provide a notion of the tasteful luxury that the Hohenzollern family once enjoyed here. The most representative room, the luminous White Salon, is both stark and elegant with its white-on-white decor punctuated by Schinkel-inspired built-in wooden Pompeian benches and a copy of an antique Roman bust set into one wall.

Portraits of the prince and princess show a handsome and dashing couple, whose intention was to represent a high point in Prussian culture and refinement. Select pieces from a KPM porcelain dinner service, as well as some gilded, satin-covered furniture designed by Schinkel, reveal the lavish tastes of this sophisticated household.

Under the aegis of Prince Karl's wife, Princess Marie of Prussia, who was a former student of Goethe's, the summer residence was a haven for artists and scientists, including the naturalist Alexander von Humboldt, the sculptor Christian Daniel Rauch, and the painters Carl Begas and Franz Krüger. An ardent Anglophile, and an accomplished pianist, she took a keen interest in the design of the estate, working closely with the architect Ludwig Persius, who directed work on the villa in close collaboration with Schinkel.

Despite her privileged situation, the princess found that living with an ardent aesthete such as her husband could be something of a trial. It seems that the prince's tireless passion

SCHINKEL PAINTED THIS ROOM A BRILLIANT GREEN
AND DESIGNED THE SATIN-COVERED, EBONY-AND-GOLD ROMAN-STYLE COUCH.

for collecting—whether it was for weapons, jewels, antiquities, or sculptures—took precedence over everything else, including his family, much to the chagrin of his spouse. "Karl could be very despotic," notes Suzanne Fontaine, who oversees the direction of the Kleinglienicke estate. "He was away for months at a time, and spent a lot of money on his collection, to the detriment of household needs. The princess complains of this quite a bit in her letters to him."

Nonetheless, seeing the palace and gardens, brimming with Greek, Roman, and Italian statuary and fragments collected by Prince Karl on his trips to Pompeii and Carthage, it is possible to imagine delightful summer days when family members and guests would hunt, take walks, read, play music, or enjoy tea in the Great Curiosity, a circular structure in the form of an antique Greek temple overlooking Potsdam's environs as distant as Schloss Babelsberg. (The crown prince provided the initial idea of adapting the third-century B.C. monument of Lysicrates at Athens to create this circular tea pavilion.)

Those who desired even greater privacy used the Little Curiosity, a tent-shaped teahouse decorated with sarcophagus reliefs and fragments of Pompeian mosaics and frescoes, that offers a view of the dome atop Schinkel's Saint Nicholas Church in Potsdam.

By far the most enchanting creation of Schinkel's on the estate is the Casino, a two-story Italianate edifice decorated with Pompeian frescoes, and set off by extended pergolas and columned terraces. From the Casino's terraces, guests could survey the Prince's own private fleet of gaily decorated gondolas used for excursions on the Havel, which he likened to his beloved Bay of Naples. While the stucco-and-marble-decorated downstairs rooms in the Casino were once used for billiards, today

THE POLYCHROME STUCCO-AND-MARBLE ORNAMENTED DOWNSTAIRS GALLERY
IN THE CASINO, WHICH WAS ONCE USED FOR BILLIARDS, STILL CONTAINS
SOME OF PRINCE KARL'S PRIZED ANTIQUE SCULPTURES.

THE EQUESTRIAN PORTRAIT OF PRINCE KARL IN FULL MILITARY DRESS
REVEALS A MAN WHO COULD BE BOTH DASHING AND IMPOSING.

they contain some of the Prince's prized antiquities, including a Roman copy (first century A.D.) of the Greek philosopher Demosthenes.

Those visitors who trek over to the northern part of the estate will be struck by the Hunters' Gate and Lodge, built in the English Tudor style, as well as by the Devil's Bridge linking two rocky points along the Havel. While these show a marked contrast with the Neoclassical villa, they are in keeping with Schinkel's other passion, English Gothic.

Despite the damage and consequent alterations to the estate (which was turned over to the German authorities in 1934, damaged during the war, and subsequently used as a hotel until 1986), Kleinglienicke still manages to retain the aura of its glorious past.

After a day spent on this splendid estate, which might include listening to a concert in the handsomely restored Orangerie, it would be difficult to envision a more enchanting setting. It is wonderful to know that, at long last, visitors from both East and West can walk freely through the grounds of Kleinglienicke, and see that Schinkel's and Lenné's masterpiece—once situated at the crossroads of history—has beautifully withstood all of Germany's vicissitudes.

Georg Kolbe Museum

Sensburger Allee 25
14055 Berlin-Charlottenburg
Tel: 304–21–44

Open Tuesday through Sunday
10:00 A.M. to 5:00 P.M.

Bus: 149

IT is easy to pass by the handsome, unobtrusive brick-and-glass Georg Kolbe Museum located on this quiet, tree-lined residential street in Charlottenburg, south of Heerstrasse Cemetery, one of the most beautifully landscaped cemeteries in Berlin. Located in Kolbe's light-filled studio house built in 1928 by the Bauhaus-inspired Swiss architect Ernst Rentsch, the museum is a showcase for one of the most important twentieth-century German figurative sculptors, as well as works by his contemporaries Gerhard Marcks (1881–1981), Rudolf Belling (1888– 1972), and Renée Sinteris (1888–1965).

While Kolbe's reputation has been overshadowed in Germany, since non-figurative art now eclipses literal representation, this museum is

THIS EXPRESSIONIST STATUE
BY THE ARTIST POINTS THE WAY TO
THE GEORG KOLBE MUSEUM—
A LIGHT-FILLED EDIFICE BUILT IN 1928
BY THE BAUHAUS-INSPIRED
SWISS ARCHITECT ERNST RENTSCH.

KOLBE'S *DANCER IN FOUNTAIN* (1912) EXUDES SUCH UNEXPECTED ENERGY
AND INTENSITY THAT THE BRONZE STATUE SEEMS TO BE
LEAPING INTO THE AIR.
(PHOTO: GEORG KOLBE MUSEUM)

nonetheless worthy of a detour if only
to contemplate this sculptor's powerful life-size bronze male and female
nudes, which often communicate
a sense of concentrated power and
grandeur, without sacrificing delicacy
or grace. Kolbe's command over his
subject and materials compelled
German art critic Carl Georg Heise to
write in the April 1927 issue of *Art
in America:* "Is it possible that a work
of art can give full credit to the
picturesque charm of movement and
at the same time attain the sculptural
repose of definite form? Can repose

and movement be united? Kolbe's
works prove this. Kolbe's best productions are moving figures. One
never asks: what has happened before
and what will follow?—one sees only
this one phase as if it were immortal
in its measured beauty."

This "measured beauty" can be
seen in many of the outdoor
sculptures in the museum, which
demonstrate the artist's decision to
focus on the human figure, not only
as a source of energy and motion,
but also as a means of self-expression.

Born in 1877, the fourth of eight

KOLBE'S WATERCOLOR SKETCH, *RECLINING WOMAN* (1916), REVEALS THE ARTIST'S EARLY AFFINITY FOR PAINTING, AS WELL AS THE INFLUENCE OF THE ARTIST AND SCULPTOR AUGUSTE RODIN. (PHOTO: GEORG KOLBE MUSEUM)

children in a modest working-class family (his father was a master house-painter), Kolbe realized early that art would be his vocation. Although the museum's collection shows that his earliest works were paintings and watercolors, he soon turned to sculpture, later confiding "I was destined to become a sculptor." After attending the School of Arts and Crafts in Dresden, and studying at the Academy of Fine Arts in Munich, he went to Paris in 1897, where he spent a year at the renowned Académie Julien.

By 1905, Kolbe had not only become a member of the Berlin Secession (which had revolted against the rigid confines of academic paint-ing and sculpture), but had had his first exhibition at the gallery of the art dealer Paul Cassirer, who supported many other notable artists, including Max Liebermann and Käthe Kollwitz.

In 1909, he returned to Paris,

this time to visit the studio of the French sculptor Auguste Rodin. While his early work included both idealized and realistic figures, and demonstrated the influence of Greek sculpture as well as that of Rodin, by 1910 his artistic expression had come into its own. Kolbe now modeled graceful, lyrical figures, full of movement, usually young women, and sometimes exotic models. It was at this time that he established his main methods of working: modeling his figures either in clay or carving them out of plaster, and then casting them in bronze. (All the works in the museum were made in a bronze foundry, under the close supervision of Kolbe himself.)

Compared with sculptures of the previous generation, these natural-looking figures were devoid of any allegorical or social significance, and disavowed classical canons of beauty, as well. Kolbe's masterpiece from this period is *The Dancer* of 1911–12, which was acquired by the Berlin National Gallery immediately after its completion. With its outstretched arms and thrown-back head, this lithe, animalistic sculpture represented a notable departure from the static, self-contained figures that were conceived according to the academic rules of Adolf von Hildebrand, whose aim was a timeless classical purity of form.

Few observers were indifferent to this remarkable sculpture, the first work of the Berlin Secession to be acquired by a German state museum. "Who does not know her, the dancer with the floating, outstretched arms and her head thrown back dreamily, rotating on soft, quiet soles?" wrote the art patron William R. Valentiner. "Every line of her body—of both outline and inner area—leads around the figure and creates a feeling of real life."

"In *The Dancer* he created a very high work of art, instinct with personality and beauty," opined the art critic Stanley Casson, in an article entitled "The Recent Development of George Kolbe," published in the August 1930 issue of *International Studio.* "*The Dancer* reveals at once an acute sensibility for grace of outline and an obvious predilection for simplicity."

While Kolbe's visit to Egypt around 1913 inspired him to create simplified and more compact figures, such as *The Dancer Nijinsky,* (1913–19), in the decade following World War I, his sculpture reflected Expressionistic and Cubist influences, something that his friendship with the painter Karl Schmidt-Rottluff undoubtedly encouraged. Among the significant works from this period in the museum are *Figure for Fountain, Assunta, Dancer for Fountain, Large Kneeling Nude,* and *Proclamation* (the memorial to booksellers who had died in World War I).

By the mid-Twenties, Kolbe had resumed making more natural and less stylized sculptures. His figures became more severe and stark than those executed prior to World War I, and their surface was both rougher and more impressionistic. At the same time, he was increasingly compelled to sculpt self-contained and serene female nudes, standing, kneeling, and sitting. After the early death of his wife, Benjamine, in 1927, he produced a number of figures showing sorrow and melancholy, such as *Pietà* and *Solitary.* While these sculptures

THIS TABLETOP SCULPTURE,
SPRING (1912),
BY GERHARD MARKS
SHOWS THE CONCENTRATION
AND THRUST OF A LEAPING MAN
FROZEN IN TIME.
(PHOTO: GEORG KOLBE MUSEUM)

YOUNG DROMEDARY
BY RENEE SINTERIS (1927)
HAS AN UNEXPECTED PERKINESS
AND LIGHTNESS
NOT NORMALLY ASSOCIATED WITH
THIS ANIMAL.
(PHOTO: GEORG KOLBE MUSEUM)

more important to him than facial features."

As was the case for many artists of his generation, Kolbe's art stagnated with the rise of National Socialism in Germany. During this period, he produced mostly athletic male nudes, in accordance with the aesthetic ideals of the Nazi regime. "For the National Socialists, the naked man repeated the classical ideal of the heroic athlete in his naturalness," writes Peter Adam in *Art of the Third Reich*. Although at the outset of the Nazi regime Kolbe was attacked for having done monuments to the Jewish poet Heinrich Heine and the Jewish statesman Walter Rathenau, he was nonetheless soon regarded as one of the best examples of the realist school, along with his colleagues Fritz Klimsch (1870–1960) and Richard Scheibe (1879–1964), prompting a leading art historian to assert: "We know that we owe to these three masters the salvation of a strong German form in the midst of decadence."

Yet, even if Kolbe's nude sculptures satisfied the National Socialist notions of male beauty, he refused to be drawn into the regime's monument-making excesses, preferring instead to continue producing work that remained on a human scale. Unlike Arno Breker and Josef Thorak, he turned down the opportunity to become an official artist of the Third Reich, and declined a commission to do a portrait bust of Hitler. (However, he did do a portrait of the Spanish dictator Franco.) The only larger-than-life-size figures he produced during the Third Reich was the *Ring of Statues*, a circle of pillars and sculptures erected in Frankfurt, in the Rothschild Park. After the war, he produced only a few more sculptures, some of them with new themes, the most famous one being entitled *Liberated*.

are quite moving, the same cannot be said for his statuesque male nudes from this period, which tend to be stiff and forbidding.

As the most prominent sculptor of his time, Kolbe was constantly busy with commissions for portrait busts of famous artists, writers, and statesmen, such as the architect Henry van der Velde, the painter Max Liebermann, and the Socialist Friedrich Ebert, as well as memorials to Heine and Beethoven. While these portraits were generally acknowledged to be good likenesses, they did not garner the same acclaim as his other works. This is not surprising, considering his preference for the human body over the face. "Kolbe searched for expression through movement, because he believed that you could show feeling through the body," notes Dr. Ursel Berger, the museum's curator. "The body's movement was always

While a number of critics within Germany, as well as beyond her borders, believe Kolbe's association with the Nazis has permanently tarnished his posthumous reputation, few dispute his genius, which established him as one of the most important German sculptors in the Twenties, as well as among the most successful. He is best remembered today as one of those influential sculptors of this century who, along with Rodin and Maillol, masterfully employed the human figure to express their ideas and feelings.

Perhaps it is the critic Albert Hentzen who best understood the sculptor's private reality, when he wrote in 1930: "Kolbe's art is closer to Nature than that of nearly all his contemporaries. His calm female nudes breathe a living warmth. . . . But it is not the character of our age as we generally see it that lives in Kolbe's art. Like many artists today, he has created his own world around him." Today, thanks to the Georg Kolbe museum, it is possible to discover the beautiful, sensuous world that he was inspired to create and which has left such a lasting mark on figurative sculpture.

THIS SILVER AND GOLD-VERMEIL *ELEPHANT WARRIOR*
BY CHRISTOPHER JAMNITZER OF NUREMBERG, (C. 1600)
WAS INTENDED TO REPLICATE HANNIBAL'S ELEPHANTS CROSSING THE ALPS.
(PHOTO: STAATLICHE MUSEEN PREUSSISCHER KULTURBESITZ, KUNSTGEWERBEMUSEUM, BERLIN).

Museum of Applied Arts

Tiergartenstrasse 6
Kulturforum
D-10785 Berlin (Tiergarten)
Tel: 266–29–02

Open Tuesday through Friday
10:00 A.M. to 6:00 P.M.
Saturday and Sunday
11:00 A.M. to 6:00 P.M.

S-Bahn: 1 to Potsdamer Platz
U-Bahn: 2 to Potsdamer Platz
Bus: 129, 148, 248

Cafeteria on premises.

I N the middle of the sixteenth century, cultivated and wealthy Germanic princes prided themselves on the magnificence of their art cabinets, known as *Kunstschrank*. Lavishly decorated with silver strapwork, pilasters, finials, shells, masks, cherubims, lions' heads, sphinxes, gods and goddesses, these massive Mannerist ebony chests, which contained priceless natural and man-made objects, often of great rarity, were intended to enchant and amuse their owners, as well as to demonstrate a prince's power and cultural attainments.

Visitors to the Museum of Applied Arts in the heart of Berlin's Kulturforum are bound to be dazzled

THE STARKLY MODERN EDIFICE OF THE KUNSTGEWERBEMUSEUM,
DESIGNED BY ROLF GUTBROD AND BUILT ACROSS FROM THE PHILARMONIE
BETWEEN 1978 AND 1985,
DOMINATES THE AREA OF BERLIN KNOWN AS THE KULTURFORUM.

by the sight of several such cabinets, as well as by the remarkable array of objects from the sixteenth-century *Pommersche Kunstschrank* produced by Philipp Hainhofer of Augsburg. Although this legendary cabinet was destroyed by bombs during World War II, one can still admire its extant riches, which include exquisite astronomical, mathematical, and surgical instruments; precious wood and ivory combs; and silver pieces for various games, the rules for many of which have been either lost or forgotten.

The *pièce de résistance* of the *Pommersche Kunstschrank* remains the elegant ivory chessboard engraved with vignettes depicting different aspects of a sinful, upside-down universe: a naked woman trapped in a birdcage, a monk gambling with dice, a donkey playing backgammon, a fox teaching a goose her ABCs. The chessboard represented a dangerous

world without rules and contrasted sharply with the chess game itself, which is played according to fixed rules in a finite world, exemplified by the chess set's silver-embossed ebony frame, which is decorated with the four continents (Europe, Asia, America, and Africa) and the four elements (earth, air, fire, and water).

While visitors are enthralled by the exquisite artistry of each object in this *Kunstschrank*, few are aware that the German prince who commissioned it believed that the art cabinet and its contents represented a wondrous microcosm of the world, intended for contemplation and reflection. In his 1565 treatise on organizing a *Kunstkammer* (the prince's treasury where such art cabinets were kept), the artistic counselor to the Duke of Bavaria, Samuel Quiccheberg, wrote that such a collection was "a vast theater of remarkable substances and exemplary likenesses representing the totality of things." Since the *Kunstkammer* and the *Kunstschrank* were meant to enlighten the prince regarding the laws of nature and science, it was widely assumed that their contents could endow a ruler with special powers, and might even help him to be a more effective sovereign.

Only a select coterie was allowed to glimpse the *Kunstschrank* and its contents as long as it remained in the Prince's possession. It wouldn't be until the close of the nineteenth century that the general public was permitted to view these rare and precious objects, largely as a result of an initiative taken by the Crown Prince of Prussia, Frederick III, and his wife Vicki, Queen Victoria's eldest daughter. Realizing that the superlative craftsmanship that had distinguished Germany's decorative arts for centuries was being diminished by the onslaught of the Industrial Revolution, the royal couple urged

THIS FORMAL DINNER SERVICE (SHOWN IN A SPECIAL EXHIBITION),
INCLUDES A SET OF LIGHT-GREEN URANIUM GLASS. IT WAS PART OF THE WEDDING
TROUSSEAU OF THE PRINCESS ALEXANDRA NIKOLAEVNA, DAUGHTER OF TSAR NICHOLAS I.
(PHOTO: STAATLICHE MUSEEN PREUSSISCHER KULTURBESITZ,
KUNSTGEWERBEMUSEUM, BERLIN)

the creation of a museum dedicated to the applied arts, which would be modeled after the recently opened Victoria & Albert Museum in London. It was thought that by exposing workers and entrepreneurs to the Hohenzollern's outstanding collections of textiles, glassware, porcelain, and precious metalwork, factories would produce commercially viable objects that reflected the German Empire's rich artistic heritage.

The forerunner of the present-day Kunstgewerbemuseum was the Royal Museum of Decorative Art, founded in 1867 around the *Brandischer Kunstkammer.* Thanks to a donation by the German Emperor William I, this collection boasted a total of 7,000 objects, including tapestries, ceramics and glassware, and highly ornate metalwork made of gold, silver, and precious stones. Until 1920, the collection was housed in the Martin Gropius Bau, a handsome Neo-Renaissance edifice built between 1877 and 1881 by Heino Schmieden and Martin Gropius, a great uncle of the Bauhaus architect Walter Gropius. Endowed with a munificent budget, the museum's first director, Julius Lessing, spent three decades scouring England, Italy, France, and Turkey, in pursuit of the finest works of applied art made between the

Middle Ages and 1900.

"Before the war this museum had a collection of 80,000 pieces," notes Dr. Barbara Mundt, its director. "In

1939, the museum's staff buried the most valuable pieces in caves beneath the Berlin City Palace. The city palace was bombed, and only a small part of the collections survived. We lost almost our entire holdings of stained-glass, textiles, glassware, majolica, and faïence, as well as much of our jewelry. It was the greatest loss ever recorded in the field of decorative arts. Today, our museum has about 40,000 pieces, and that includes 8,000 acquisitions since the war."

After the war, the remaining applied arts collections were split up, finding new homes in East or West Berlin, depending upon the site of their wartime storage. In West Berlin, a provisional museum was installed inside the Charlottenburg Palace,

until the present modern building, designed by Rolf Gutbrod and built across from the Berlin Philharmonic between 1978 and 1985, had been completed. Built for small objects, the four-story museum is mainly dedicated to European applied arts, with a strong emphasis on the Middle Ages, the Renaissance, as well as the Neoclassical, Victorian, and Bauhaus periods. (In East Berlin, the other part of the collection, mainly furniture and the huge silver buffet from the Royal Palace, is normally displayed at the Baroque Palace of Berlin-Köpenik. While this palace is closed for renovations key objects are shown at the Kunstgewerbemuseum.)

The focal point of the department of Medieval applied arts is the *Welfenschatz,* the astounding treasures of the Guelph family, ancestors of England's Hanoverian dynasty, who used to figure among the most prominent landowners in Germany. Formerly kept in the Cathedral of Brunswick, this unique collection of thirty-five priceless gold and silver reliquaries made between the eleventh and fifteenth centuries includes the celebrated Domed Reliquary in the form of a Byzantine church, adorned with exquisite ivory carvings and enamelling (Cologne, c. 1175), the Byzantine-style portable altar of Eilbertus made of rock crystal and semi-precious stones (Cologne, c. 1150), an eleventh-century, diamond and gem-studded crucifix (*Welfenkreuz*), as well as a fourteenth-century bookcover made of jasper, rock crystal, and parchment miniatures of courtly and mythological scenes. (When the Guelph treasure appeared on the market in the early 1930s, after the family had lost its sovereignty, this remarkable collection barely escaped being sold piecemeal to different museums around the world. Recognizing the treasure's exceptional value and artistry, the Cultural Ministry raised the requisite sum needed to acquire the *Welfenschatz*, even going so far as to sell other works of art to pay for it, including a painting by Cimabue.)

Just as outstanding are the objects from the Medieval Basel Cathedral treasure, including the baptismal font of the Emperor Frederick I Barbarossa (c. 1160), and the early eleventh-century *Heinrichskreuz* (Henry Cross), the reliquary crucifix of Emperor Henry II.

In the adjoining rooms are a series of six Brussels tapestries woven around 1530, based on Petrarch's *Trionfo*, representing Chastity, Love, Fame, Time, Death, and the Triumph of God over the universe. The highlight of the collection however, is the finest array of Renaissance silverware in existence, which includes the complete set of municipal silverware of the Hanseatic city of Lüneburg, whose wealth was amassed from the salt mines in the Harz Mountains: thirty-three pieces in all, each one more elaborately crafted and gilded than the next, with scenes and symbols from the Old and New Testament, as well as mythological deities.

"For centuries this silver was kept in a wooden cupboard in the Lüneburg Town Hall, and was used for important diplomatic receptions and feast days," notes Dr. Mundt. "The city fathers who had donated these objects ruled in the fifteenth century that they should only be sold in times of greatest need. They maintained that position even through the Thirty Years' War, which devastated Germany." However, by the nineteenth century, with its former wealth vastly depleted, Lüneburg's municipal government was forced to sell its legendary silver collection in 1873 to raise money to build a modern septic system—a decision that provoked a huge outcry from the city's leading families.

No visitor should overlook the masterful creations by the goldsmiths from Nuremberg and Augsburg, in particular the Imperial Goblet by Wenzel Jamnitzer and the Elephant

THIS ELEGANT EBONY AND IVORY CHESSBOARD FROM THE POMMERSCHER KUNSTSCHRANK, AUGSBURG (1610–16), ILLUSTRATES DIFFERENT FACETS OF A SINFUL, UPSIDE-DOWN UNIVERSE. (PHOTO: STAATLICHE MUSEEN PREUSSISCHER KULTURBESITZ, KUNSTGEWERBEMUSEUM, BERLIN)

Hunt by his nephew, Christopher. Wenzel Jamnitzer was one of the most eminent goldsmiths of the sixteenth century; not only was his ornate Mannerist style highly influential, but he was also reputedly the first craftsman to have used the moresque style as a form of ornamentation, and the first to exploit the technique of etching to decorate silver.

Even with much of its former collection irretrievably lost during the war, the calm and handsomely organized Kunstgewerbemuseum still offers an embarrassment of riches. Happily, one need no longer be a German princeling or a privileged member of his entourage in order to contemplate and enjoy some of Europe's most spellbinding treasures.

Lutherhalle Wittenberg

Luther's Hall Wittenberg

Collegienstrasse 54
D-06886 Lutherstadt Wittenberg
Tel: (0–34–91) 40–26–71

**Open Tuesday through Sunday
9:00 A.M. to 5:00 P.M.**

**By train: Take the train from
Lichtenberg station to Wittenberg;
then take a bus or taxi to the
museum.**

WHEN Martin Luther
(1483–1546) arrived in Wittenberg
in the fall of 1508 to fill the chair
of moral philosophy at the Saxon-
Ernestine State University, he moved
into the town's Augustinian
monastery, built by the Elector
Frederick the Wise between 1503
and 1507. In one of his discourses,
which was later recorded in the
famed *Table Talk*, he complained:
"We are sitting here in drudgery . . .
at the edge of civilization . . . in the
midst of barbarism."

It was hard for this miner's son
to imagine that, within less than ten
years after his arrival in Wittenberg,
this sleepy town would become
the center of an unprecedented

THE LUTHERHALLE IN WITTENBERG,
A FORMER SIXTEENTH-CENTURY AUGUSTINIAN MONASTERY,
WAS SAVED FROM FALLING INTO DECAY, BY THE INTERVENTION OF THE ARCHITECT
SCHINKEL. HIS PUPIL AND SUCCESSOR, FRIEDRICH AUGUST STÜLER,
RECONSTRUCTED THE EDIFICE, IN THE NEO-GOTHIC STYLE, FROM 1844 TO 1873.

THIS STATUE OF MARTIN LUTHER, ERECTED IN 1821,
OVERLOOKS WITTENBERG TOWN HALL AND THE TOWN CHURCH,
AS WELL AS THE CITY'S MARKETPLACE.

theological firestorm, one which would not only challenge the Pope's authority, but would also lead to fundamental social changes that would pave the way for the modern nation-state.

This pivotal point in history, with all its attendant drama and complexity, is illustrated through rare original documents and artwork by such masters as Lucas Cranach the Elder and Albrecht Dürer, in an encyclopedic exhibition at Luther's Hall in Wittenberg. Located in the former sixteenth-century Augustinian monastery, this museum has all the pedagogical features of a modern institution (including an interactive computer station equipped with a CD-ROM). Thanks to an excellent written presentation, visitors can learn

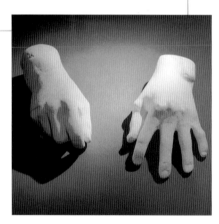

about all the major events that took place during Luther's thirty-eight years in Wittenberg, first as a dispirited monk, later as a rebel against the Roman Catholic Church, and finally as an admired, albeit controversial theologian in the service of the Saxon prince-elector.

The extensive examples of original correspondence between Luther and his contemporaries—from both friends and enemies—as well as the rich hoard of printed tracts and pamphlets, make the Luther Hall the world's largest museum on the Reformation. "We have 50,000 documents from the period, including an exceptional collection of beautiful pamphlets that Luther printed during his lifetime," notes Dr. Martin True, the Luther Hall's director. "However, due to limitations of space we can only present about five percent of what we own at any one time."

The term "Protestant work ethic" could easily be attributed to the German theologian, whose collected works were published in a 102-volume critical edition in 1883. Apart from his teaching post at the University of Wittenberg, and his duties as preacher at Saint Mary's Parish Church, Luther also wrote more than 5,000 tracts and pamphlets, all of which were printed and disseminated during his lifetime.

The exhibition's dark brown walls and elegant spot-lit vitrines (installed in 1983 to mark the 400th anniversary of Luther's birth and the centenary of the museum's opening) provide a sober backdrop for what is tantamount to a sensational drama. Beneath the austere and resolute physiognomy depicted by Lucas Cranach the Elder (the artist is said to have produced 2,000 portraits of Luther in his Wittenberg workshop), was a man with deep-seated convictions and passions. As he prepared his sermons, he came to believe that only *faith* in God can lead to one's ultimate salvation. These deep stirrings of religiosity coincided with a nadir in the Church's reputation. In 1509, Luther visited Rome and was shocked by the warrior-pope Julius II, who rode into battle in full armor and who was planning to rebuild Saint Peter's through the sale of "indulgences"—paper certificates offering relief from punishment in Purgatory.

Luther's doctrine of "justification by faith alone" was in complete opposition to the Pope's lucrative traffic in indulgences. The Augustinian monk's anger reached the boiling point when a German friar began selling indulgences in Wittenberg, despite a ban from the Elector of Saxony, who had no interest in seeing large sums pouring into the papal coffers. On All Saints Eve in 1517,

summer of 1518. Undaunted by this papal pressure, the recalcitrant Luther not only refused to recant, but dared to publicly burn the Papal Bull of Excommunication on December 10, 1520.

The Holy Roman Emperor, Charles V, who foresaw that the monk's dissidence could undermine

THE FAMOUS THESES DOORS REPLACED THE FORMER MAIN ENTRANCE
OF WITTENBERG'S PALACE CHURCH. THE BRONZE DOORS, WHICH WERE CAST IN 1858, ARE INSCRIBED
WITH LUTHER'S 95 THESES IN LATIN, *AGAINST THE DOCTRINE OF INDULGENCES*,
FIRST PRINTED ON OCTOBER 31, 1517.

Luther took the fateful step of publishing his ninety-five theses "Against the Doctrine of Indulgences," supposedly nailing them to Wittenberg's castle church door.

It was a challenge tantamout to heresy. As news of Luther's theses spread to Nuremberg, Leipzig, and Basel, a heresy trial opened against the monk in Rome during the

the relationship between church and state, summoned Luther to the Diet of Worms in March 1521 in order to justify himself before the Emperor and the Estates. Again, Luther refused to retract, "because it is neither useful nor salutary to act against conscience." Outlawed by the German Emperor, who ordered that his books be burned, Luther sought the protection of the Duke of Saxony,

Frederick the Wise. Living in hiding for a year at Wartburg Castle, he translated the New Testament from Greek into German in eleven weeks. Originally illustrated with engravings by Lucas Cranach the Elder, it is universally regarded as the first important work in modern German literature.

The museum's most precious document is a four-page manuscript letter the embattled monk sent to Charles V after the meeting at Worms, justifying his dissent. A gift from the American financier, J. Pierpoint Morgan, to Kaiser Wilhelm II, it was donated to the museum before World War I. "Morgan wanted to become a German nobleman, and obtain the Order of the Black Eagle," explains Dr. True. "The only way for him to achieve this was to make a munificent gift to the German Empire. He saw this letter as his chance. Not only did he vastly overpay for the letter, but the Kaiser only consented to give him the Order of the Red Eagle, which is given to all Prussian civil servants after twenty-five years."

Luther's demands for church reform led to the dissolution of the Augustinian monastery by January 1522. The Duke of Saxony not only turned over the monastery to Luther, but entrusted him with reorganizing the church system. Dr. True maintains that the Duke of Saxony gave him this authority because of his intellectual renown, which had helped make the University of Wittenberg the largest in Europe. (It did not hurt that Luther was vehemently opposed to the violent social disturbances during the Peasants' War of 1524–25, and backed the status quo.)

The reformer was soon busy with church inspections, the secularization of monasteries and seminaries, the establishment of salaries for preachers and educators, as well as a community welfare system for the poor, and schools for both sexes. (The first girls' school in Germany opened in Wittenberg in 1529.) "Until the Reformation, only ten percent of the male population had the opportunity to go to school," notes Dr. True. "Luther changed all that. He believed you had to be educated in order to have faith."

Also known as "the nightingale of Wittenburg," Luther was an accomplished poet, musician, and composer. Endowed with a good tenor voice, he maintained that musical participation was the liturgical counterpart to his theological doctrine. The Lutheran musical tradition required for the first time that every parish support its cantor, its organist, its choir school, and its body of trained singers and instrumentalists. This requirement was to play a prominent role in making Germany the most musically educated nation in Europe. Many musicologists are convinced there is a direct link between the hymns and masses of Luther and Heinrich Schutz, and the later glories of Bach, Haydn, Mozart, Beethoven, Schubert, and Brahms.

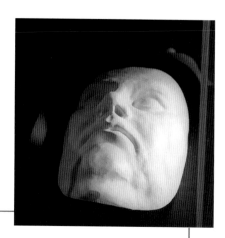

LUTHER'S DEATH MASK REVEALS A STRONG-WILLED INDIVIDUAL WITH A SET MOUTH, JUTTING CHIN, AND PUGNACIOUS NOSE.

LUTHER BUILT THIS ROOM IN 1535 BY ADDING INTERNAL WALLS TO
AN ORIGINALLY LARGER SPACE. WOODEN PANELING, REACHING UP TO THE CEILING,
PROVIDED WARMTH AND INSULATION.
THE MASSIVE BOX TABLE AND BOX SEAT AT THE WINDOW
WERE USED BY THE THEOLOGIAN.

Residing in the former Augustinian monastery, the theologian made his most visible break with monasticism. On June 13, 1525, he married the former nun Katherina von Bora, who had fled from the Nibeschen convent near Grimma; he was 43, she was 26. Their engagement and "copulation" (symbolic lying down on the nuptial bed with witnesses present) took place in the old monastery. Six children were born to the couple, of whom two died in infancy. Referred to by Luther as "Master Cathy," the highly effective and resolute Katherina brewed and sold the monastery's beer, occupied herself with farming and the acquisition of land, and ultimately amassed a sizable family fortune.

The carefully preserved "Luther's Room" permits visitors to picture some of the theologian's domestic arrangements. Already designated "Museum Lutheri" in 1655, it was shown upon request to interested visitors, including the Russian Tsar, Peter the Great, who left his autograph in white chalk over the western door. One can imagine Luther seated with his friends around the massive oak table, engrossed in a lively exchange regarding God and creation, while downing numerous steins of home-brewed beer.

While the radical theologian died before the 1555 Peace of Augsburg, when Protestantism was officially recognized in the states of northern Germany, this intriguing museum demonstrates that in his challenge to authority, in his resolute refusal to disavow his beliefs, as well as in his far-sighted social reforms, Luther's example remains inspiring and influential both within Germany and well beyond its frontiers.

Dorfmuseum Marzahn-Sammlungen
Handwerksmuseum und Friseurmuseum

Marzahn Village Museum-Collections from the Handicrafts Museum and Hairdressing Museum

Alt-Marzahn 31
12685 Berlin-Marzahn
Tel: 541–02–31

Open Tuesday through Sunday
10:00 A.M. to 6:00 P.M.

S-Bahn: 75 to Springfuhl, then
take Tram 6, 7, or 17 to Marzahn.

UNTIL almost the end of the nineteenth century, elegant ladies were coiffed at home, because Berlin had no independent hair salons catering to women. This state of affairs did not change until 1880 when François Haby opened an establishment catering to both men and women, which soon became the most fashionable and frequented hair salon in the city. Not only did this hairdresser become celebrated for his advertising slogans (his shaving cream was called "Wake-up!" and his shampoo for women was called "I can be so nice"), but he also

THE MARZAHN VILLAGE MUSEUM,
LOCATED IN THIS RESTORED ONE-HUNDRED-YEAR-OLD WOODEN FARMHOUSE,
CONTRASTS SHARPLY WITH
THE ROWS OF DREARY PUBLIC-HOUSING PROJECTS SURROUNDING IT.

concocted a hair unguent called "That does it!" that was used by Kaiser Wilhelm II to secure his renowned handlebar mustache. Soon, patriotic Germans everywhere were imitating the Kaiser's look.

The notoriously despotic and enterprising Haby became so wealthy (due in no small measure to the fact that his employees worked seven days a week and had only a single day off after a year), that he was able to commission the Belgian architect Henry van der Velde to design a sumptuous Art Nouveau salon that contained twelve seats for men and seven for women.

It's surprising to see part of this unique salon—a symbol of Wilhelmine plutocracy—in Marzahn, a working-class suburb east of Berlin, and the automotive manufacturing center of the Trabant, the former East Germany's answer to Ford's Model T. Van der Velde's sumptuous interior is just one of the many fascinating exhibits to be found at the Marzahn Village Museum, notable for its comprehensive collection devoted to the history of hairdressing, as well as for its exhibits illustrating the tools and techniques used in such manual occupations as carpentry, cabinetmaking, shoemaking, and the craft of the wheelwright. "The older people who visit this museum still remember the tools they once used to make things," notes curator Dr. Barbara Hoffmann. "The young, on the other hand, are often surprised to see how things used to be made."

Located in a one-hundred-year-old wooden farmhouse in the picturesque hamlet of Alt-Marzahn (which was rebuilt by Frederick the Great after the devastation of the Thirty Years' War, and restored by the former GDR for the 750th anniversary of Berlin), this intimate, atypical museum contrasts sharply with the rows of dreary

public-housing projects that surround it. Considering the tedium and lack of initiative in the workplace that was commonplace during the former Communist regime, one can understand why, in the 1960s, an East German hairdresser, Jörg Maiwald,

THIS OLD-FASHIONED BARBERSHOP
FEATURES A SHELF OF
NUMBERED SHAVING MUGS THAT
BELONGED TO DIFFERENT PATRONS WHO
CAME IN DAILY TO BE SHAVED.

might have amassed artifacts and documents associated with the glamorous and unusual aspects of hairdressing.

Stored in his cellar, the collection attracted the attention of the East German hairdressers trade union, which eventually assumed control over it and presented it to the public in 1987 within a museum located in Berlin's Prenslauerberg section. After the unification of Germany in 1990, the collection came under the jurisdiction of the Markisches Museum (East Berlin's city museum) and, in 1994, it was transferred to its present location in Alt-Marzahn. The handicrafts collection was added at this time and installed in the attic of an outbuilding.

While the museum's principal emphasis is on the history and evolution of hairdressing in Germany (including in the former GDR), it also provides a fascinating global overview of the profession since Antiquity. Perhaps no other line of work has involved so many different types of disciplines, including barbering, hairdressing, wig-making, cosmetology, medicine, surgery, dentistry, and theatrical hairstyling.

Some barbers have also been ingenious inventors and remarkable statesmen. For instance, in 1769 the English barber Richard Arkwright (1732–1792), devised a spinning machine—the water frame—which led to the establishment of huge cotton mills and the factory system. The Polish barber Stanislaw Staszic (1755–1828), rose to become a noted scientist and statesman, and later gave his millions to scientific institutions and to the peasants whom he liberated from serfdom.

A small collection of tweezers, razors, bronze mirrors, and cosmetic palettes from ancient Egypt (c. 2500–1800 B.C.) demonstrates that hairdressing and wig-making have been established professions since the Fourth Dynasty (c. 2600 B.C.) Elaborate wigs and beards made of human and animal hair were *de rigueur* at court. Even high-ranking *women* donned fake beards to demonstrate that they commanded as much authority as men.

The code of Hammurabi, the oldest written compendium of laws, not only demonstrates that both barbers

THIS RECONSTRUCTED WORKSHOP
OF A GERMAN COBBLER
WITH ITS ASSORTED TOOLS, SHOES, AND LASTS
IS STRAIGHT OUT OF A GRIMM'S FAIRY TALE.

THIS DISPLAY OF FISHERMAN'S GEAR,
INCLUDING LANTERNS, NETS, WEIGHTS, AND FISH LURES,
PAYS NOSTALGIC TRIBUTE TO A FORMER WAY OF LIFE.

and doctors practiced surgery in Babylon, but includes warnings against their possible malpractice and abuse of power. If a patient did not survive an operation, the physicians could have their hands cut off!

In ancient Greece, where professional barbers had been active since the fourth century B.C., long, fair tresses and complicated hairstyles were the height of fashion. Customers who were not naturally blond had their hair lightened with a variety of alkaline bleaches imported from Phoenicia. Others had their hair dusted with a talc mixture made of yellow pollen, yellow flour, and fine gold dust. Roman men, on the other hand, eschewed fair tresses in favor of dark or black hair, which was often darkened with hair dyes, including one made from boiled walnut shells and leeks.

During the Middle Ages,

European barbers and bath attendants worked in public bath houses, the precursors of modern beauty salons. Although organized into guilds by the fourteenth century, they did not enjoy an enviable social position. Not only were barbers viewed with disdain and ranked alongside executioners and night-watchmen, they also were not allowed to bear arms, nor were their children allowed to engage in certain professions. While the King of Bohemia, Wenceslas IV (who supported the Czech religious reformer Jan Hus), issued an edict in 1406 declaring that barbering was an honest profession, it wasn't until 1548 that Augsburg's Reichstag determined that the barbers' guild was entitled to the same status as other corporations.

After the Church banned the clergy from performing surgery in the Middle Ages, barbers also became

THE ART NOUVEAU BELGIAN ARCHITECT HENRY VAN DER VELDE
DESIGNED THE SUMPTUOUS UNISEX HAIRDRESSING SALON FOR FRANÇOIS HABY,
AT ONE TIME THE MOST FAMOUS HAIRDRESSER IN GERMANY.

surgeons and physicians. The museum's collection of ceramic bleeding bowls, apothecary jars, skulls, and other medical paraphenalia, illustrates the dual nature of the barber's profession. Besides being responsible for simple interventions, such as bleeding, teeth-pulling, and dressing wounds, they were also permitted to amputate, treat battle wounds, and later conduct autopsies. Georg Bartisch, the son of a bath attendant and himself a barber at Gräfenheim near Dresden, was not only a celebrated surgeon, but the Duke of Saxony's personal oculist. In 1583, he published a book on the physiology of the eye, thus precipitating the development of ophthalmology.

Displays of antique dental equipment, fillings, and false teeth show that German barbers also cleaned and filled teeth from the Middle Ages until the first third of this century. Unfortunately, the numerous charlatans who pulled teeth at country fairs were responsible for the negative image that was attributed to even those reputable barbers who also practiced legitimate dentistry.

Among the museum's most unexpected exhibits is a wig-makers atelier, complete with finished and unfinished wigs, wooden rollers, and stretchers for flattening and curling the hair. While wigs were commonplace in the ancient world, they were periodically banned by the Church, which argued that the teachings of Jesus and the Apostles opposed all artifice. By the seventeenth century, however, European courts were eager to emulate the luxuriant wigs worn by Louis XIV, the Continent's most powerful monarch. While his Minister of Finance, Colbert, objected to the enormous expense of importing hair for the "Sun King's" wigs, he relented when the wig-makers guild convinced him that the revenues from French wig exports would far outweigh the costs of imported hair.

By the eighteenth century, the average Prussian courtier might pay as much as 1,000 thalers for his powdered *perruque* —a substantial sum at that time. During the Seven Years War, when Frederick the Great learned that one minister from Saxony possessed 1,500 wigs, he observed sardonically: "Quite a lot of wigs for a man without a head."

Still, no one could match the extravagant hairstyles of the French aristocracy and monarchy. Madame de Pompadour's hairdresser is said to have earned 250,000 francs a year, while Marie-Antoinette's favorite coiffeur was reportedly more highly compensated than the court's most prominent minister. Not only did the wigs worn by these highborn ladies tower over the heads of the men around them, but the heights of doorways through which they would pass had to be raised to accommodate their entrances and exits!

The museum also demonstrates the impact of women's emancipation in this century. Whereas in 1907 only eight percent of women were working as hairdressers in Germany, by 1925 women represented one-fourth of the profession. Fashionable women copied the hairdos of movie stars such as Lilian Harvey and Marlene Dietrich, or adopted the close cropped bob *(bubykopf)* of the singer/entertainer Josephine Baker.

As the only institution devoted to the history of hairdressing in Germany, the Dorf Village Museum richly demonstrates the complex past of this profession. "Our aim is to encourage respect for work accomplished with one's hands," says Dr.

Hoffman. "We also want to show that a certain intelligence was needed to produce things. By preserving these historical artifacts and documents, we make sure that these manual trades won't be lost or forgotten."

THIS RICH ARRAY OF
TORTOISESHELL AND RESIN HAIR COMBS
DEMONSTRATES THE
GLAMOROUS ORIGINALITY OF
HAIR ORNAMENTS
IN THE NINETEENTH AND EARLY
TWENTIETH CENTURY
BEFORE THE SO-CALLED "BOB"
CAME INTO FASHION.

Museum of Musical Instruments

Tiergartenstrasse 1
10785 Berlin-Tiergarten
Tel: 254–81–0

Open Tuesday through Friday
9:00 A.M. to 5:00 P.M.
Saturday and Sunday
10:00 A.M. to 5:00 P.M.

S-Bahn: 1 to Potsdamer Platz
U-Bahn: 2 to Potsdamer Platz
Bus: 129, 142, 148, 248, 341, 348

Café and concert hall on premises.

THE MUSEUM OF MUSICAL INSTRUMENTS
IN BERLIN'S KULTURFORUM
HIDES THE LANDSCAPE OF CRANES
OVERLOOKING POTSDAMMER PLATZ.
DESIGNED IN 1972 BY HANS SCHAROUN
(THE ARCHITECT OF THE BERLIN
PHILHARMONIC), THE MUSEUM
WAS COMPLETED AFTER HIS DEATH IN 1984
BY EDGAR WISNIEWSKI.

INSPIRED by the French aristocracy's predilection for the flute's soft, delicate sound, which was very much in tune with the eighteenth century's refined and sensitive spirit, Frederick the Great learned to play the instrument as a young man, and soon proved to be a talented musician and composer. So impressed was he by the Prussian monarch's virtuosity, that the English traveler Charles Burney was impelled to write: "His embouchure was clear and even, his fingering brilliant, and his taste pure and unaffected; I was much pleased, and even surprised with the neatness of his execution in the allegros, as well as by his expression and feeling in the adagio; in short, his performance surpassed, in many particulars, anything I had ever heard among Dilettanti, or even professors."

While Frederick's musical proclivity is familiar to musicologists and historians, newcomers to the Museum

THIS MID-NINETEENTH-CENTURY "SEWING-TABLE" PIANO DEMONSTRATES HOW YOUNG, GENTEEL WOMEN DIVIDED THEIR ACTIVITIES BETWEEN SEWING AND MUSIC-MAKING.

of Musical Instruments in Berlin may be surprised to discover this facet of the Prussian ruler, exemplified by an exhibit of his ebony and walrus-tooth transverse flutes shown next to a fingering chart made by his teacher, Johann Joachim Quantz. (A transverse flute features a number of interchangeable joints for the upper section of the instrument's body, which allows the pitch to be changed.) Even on the battlefield, music was never far from the Prussian monarch's thoughts, if one is to judge by the portable, folding clavichord (made by Jean Marius at the beginning of the eighteenth century), which he brought along to accompany him while he played his flute.

This tribute to Frederick's musical talent is just one of six hundred exhibits in this spacious, airy exhibition hall designed in 1972 by Hans Scharoun (the award-winning architect of Berlin's Philharmonic), and completed after his death by

Edgar Wisniewski in 1984. This intriguing museum functions as both a research institution of great benefit to instrument-makers and musicians, as well as an historical center illustrating the evolution of European music from the sixteenth through the twentieth centuries.

Set up in 1888 by the Prussian state, the museum's core collection of thirty-four instruments from the Royal Museum of Decorative Arts and 240 items that once belonged to the Leipzig publisher Paul de Wit, were incorporated into the Royal Academy of Music at the prompting of Philipp Spitta, the famous Bach biographer, and the violinist Joseph Joachim. By the 1920s, under the direction of the celebrated musicologist Curt Sachs, the museum's holdings had increased to over 3,200 items. Thanks to his unerring sense for the unusual, the collection was expanded to include a fine example of an early-eighteenth-century racket, of which only a few examples survive (this is a woodwind instrument, shaped like a cylindrical can, that sounds like an oboe), as well as twenty-four instruments for a gamelan orchestra, formerly owned by a Javanese sultan.

Regrettably, despite his remarkable publications, including his *Lexicon of Musical Instruments* (considered one of the cornerstones of twentieth-century musicology), the Jewish-born Sachs was relieved of all his duties on September 30, 1933, and was forced shortly thereafter to emigrate from Germany. Worse was to come: although evacuation of the museum's precious holdings (then located in the Palais Kreutz in the Klosterstrasse) was begun in 1943, most of the priceless collection remained in Berlin and was destroyed by bombing.

Barely 700 of the almost 4,000 instruments survived, and many of these were in terrible condition.

Knowing the hapless fate of this unparalleled collection, it seems all the more remarkable that, after the war, its decimated holdings were painstakingly reassembled to the extent that today, it comprises 2,500 instruments of international repute. Moreover, the museum's conservation department succeeded in restoring a large portion of the remaining core collection to its original state. Today, the museum's 32,000 square feet of exhibition space spread over three floors permits visitors to study the collection at their leisure, listen through headphones to classical music from specially produced compact discs, or discover the playing of an eighteenth-century clavichord or pianoforte thanks to demonstrations and concerts that are given throughout the year. A high point of any visit is being able to listen to accomplished musicians play pieces of classical music that were specifically written for the instruments on display.

"Our aim in this museum is to show visitors the uniqueness of facture and sound that is characteristic of old instruments," notes Dr. Konstantin Restle, the museum's director. "What people don't often realize is that musicians not only knew how to compose, but they often influenced the making of instruments to obtain the sound and tone they desired."

The museum possesses an extraordinary array of instruments used for sacred, courtly, and popular music, including elegant seventeenth-century Venetian and Viennese lutes, rare Baroque reed woodwinds, eighteenth-century brass hunting horns and processional trumpets, pocket violins once employed by French dancing masters, mechanical musical clocks

THIS THREE-MANUAL SLIDER-CHEST ORGAN WITH RÜCKPOSITIV WAS BUILT
BETWEEN 1815 AND 1820 BY THE LONDON FIRM OF JOHN GRAY FOR A CHURCH IN
BATHAMPTON NEAR BATH IN SOMERSET, ENGLAND.

(one late-eighteenth-century flute-playing cylinder clock by Christian Ernst Kleemeyer features an original allegretto composed by Mozart), a Biedermeier "sewing table" piano and a violin in the form of a walking stick, as well as a 1929 Wurlitzer cinema organ, once owned by Werner Ferdinand von Siemens, grandson of the Siemens Company's founder.

Its outstanding collection of rare stringed keyboard instruments from the seventeenth through the twentieth century, includes a few which were presumably played by celebrated composers such as Johann Sebastian

Bach and Wolfgang Amadeus Mozart. (Stringed instuments whose sound is produced by a key-depressing mechanism appeared only in the second half of the fourteenth century.)

Until the middle of the eighteenth century, there were two kinds of stringed keyboard instruments: those whose strings were struck, like the clavichord, and those whose strings were plucked by quills, such as the harpsichord, the spinet, and the virginal. Their lavish decoration shows they were intended to please the eye as well as the ear. There was no restriction on what a customer might request in the way of special features, including rich ornamentation and carvings, precious paintings, and costly inlaid work.

Among the earliest Flemish keyboard instruments in the museum are four harpsichords made between 1570 and 1660 by the Antwerp-based Ruckers family, widely regarded as being among the period's finest instruments, because of their incomparably sweet and silvery tone. On one particularly magnificent single-manual harpsichord by Andreas Rucker the Elder, whose soundboard depicts a garden with flowers, fruits, birds, and butterflies, one can see the date 1618 and the Biblical inscription *Soli Deo Gloria* (Glory Be To God Alone), frequently found in Johann Sebastian Bach's sacred compositions written a century later.

The collection also reflects Vienna's musical apogee, when Haydn, Mozart, and Beethoven were composing for the *Hämmerflugel* or pianoforte, which was to supersede the harpsichord and clavichord in the eighteenth century. The museum boasts a rare 1775 pianoforte made in Augsburg by Johann Andreas Stein, whose celebrated Viennese action

THESE SPLENDID CLAVICHORDS AND HARPSICHORDS,
NOTABLE FOR THEIR RICH ORNAMENTATION, FINE PAINTINGS, INTRICATE INLAID WORK,
AND ELABORATELY CARVED SOUNDBOARD ROSES,
JUSTIFY THE INSCRIPTION ON A SIXTEENTH-CENTURY ITALIAN HARPSICHORD
"I DELIGHT BOTH THE EYE AND THE HEART."

THIS FOUR-SIDED MUSIC STAND FOR CHAMBER CONCERTS WAS MADE DURING THE BIEDERMEIER ERA, WHEN THE SOCIAL CULTURE LEANED TOWARD SELF-IMPROVEMENT AND ENCOURAGED MUSICAL EVENINGS IN A DOMESTIC SETTING.

gave the player more optimal tone control, thanks to an improved damping mechanism. Mozart was so enthused about the Stein mechanism that in 1770 he wrote his father: "This time I shall begin straight away with Stein's fortepianos. I much prefer these because they damp ever so much better. In whatever way I touch the keys, the tone is always even."

The pianoforte would not only enhance an artist's playing, it would also inspire musical composition. Visitors can see the Viennese-made Joseph Brodmann pianoforte which Franz Schubert used to compose parts of his 1821 *Freischutz (The Marksman)*, regarded as Germany's first Romantic opera. The other significant maker of pianofortes with a Viennese action was Conrad Graf. Among the composers who played on Graf pianofortes were Beethoven, Liszt, and Chopin; in fact, the Polish-born composer presented Robert and Clara Schumann with a Graf pianoforte as a wedding present.

The most valuable instrument in the collection is one of the least adorned—a 1703 violin made by Antonio Stradivari of Cremona (c. 1644–1737) worth over one million DM—one of forty such violins known to exist in the world today. The Stradivarius violin, which has been played by such virtuosos as Joseph Joachim, Fritz Kreisler, and Sir Isaac Stern, is recognizable by its unique facture, particularly its varnish, which is said to influence the instrument's tonal quality. Stradivari, a master in all departments of his trade, made an unequaled varnish that gives the violin its orange-brown glow as well as a great elasticity—resulting in an instrument, which according to Joachim, "combined sweetness and grandeur."

Thanks to such scholarly exhibits and delightful musical performances, Europe's rich musical legacy comes alive in this exceptional institution. Knowing some of the fascinating history and hauntingly beautiful compositions these instruments have inspired and performed over the centuries, one is compelled to agree that music may truly be the most universal and soul-satisfying of all the arts.

Normannenstrasse Research and Memorial Center

Haus 1
Ruschestrasse 59
10365 Berlin-Lichtenberg
Tel: 553-68-54

Open Tuesday through Friday
11:00 A.M. to 6:00 P.M.
Saturday and Sunday
2:00 P.M. to 6:00 P.M.

U-Bahn: 5 to Magdalenenstrasse

THE NORMANNENSTRASSE RESEARCH
AND MEMORIAL CENTER IS LOCATED IN THE
FORMER HEADQUARTERS COMPLEX
OF THE STASI, WHERE 33,000 PEOPLE USED
TO WORK IN GATHERING BOTH
DOMESTIC AND FOREIGN INTELLIGENCE.

DURING the 1970s and the 1980s the Stasi (the former German Democratic Republic's Ministry of State Security) engaged in street-fighting and parachuting exercises in order to prepare for an invasion of West Berlin. Since there had been no Allied opposition to the building of the Berlin Wall, the Stasi's leaders had persuaded themselves that they could successfully take over West Berlin with the assistance of West German informers, and the military support of the National People's Army (as well as the Soviet Red Army). Their intention was to strike with artillery first, before unleashing the army and a pinpoint bombing campaign upon the western half of the city. So certain were they of the success of their plan, that they had already selected the location and the personnel for the new Stasi district units they intended to establish in West Berlin.

This terrifying plot, which fortunately never came to fruition (since the Stasi never obtained the necessary approval from the Soviet regime), is documented in one of this city's most singular museums, which lays bare the Orwellian nightmare of a society that was condemned to live for four decades under near-total surveillance. Innocuously named the Normannenstrasse Research and Memorial Center, the institution is run by a private association called ASTAK (Anti-Stalinist Action), that includes members of the citizen's committee that stormed the State Security Service's headquarters in January 1990.

The museum's locale is in the former headquarters complex of the

TWO STATUES, ONE OF VLADIMIR ILYICH LENIN, THE OTHER OF FELIX DZERZHINSKY (THE FOUNDER OF THE CHEKA—THE FORERUNNER TO THE KGB), STAND LIKE SENTINELS IN THE LOBBY OF THE FORMER STATE MINISTRY OF SECURITY'S HEADQUARTERS IN BERLIN.

Stasi, where 33,000 people used to work in both domestic and foreign intelligence. Once protected by a massive wall equipped with security cameras in order to observe the people who went in and out, this compound was a city in itself, with a bank, hospital, shopping center, and two restaurants, one for employees, and one for officers. Located in Building One (built in the typical Stalinist style with marble from Hitler's former chancellory), the museum documents not only the Stasi's oppressive and terrifying role in the former GDR, but also reveals the courageous resistance of dissident organizations and individuals, ranging from church-based grassroots groups to noted artists and musicians, all of whom dared to criticize and defy the omnipresent totalitarian regime.

"The people who promoted the saving of this institution are among the citizens who suffered the most from the Stasi," notes Maria-Theresia Pupke, the memorial's director of education. "This museum exists to explain the role the Stasi played in the former GDR. Because it is located in their former headquarters, this is a living history class."

Established in 1950, six months after the founding of the German Democratic Republic, the Stasi was in charge of both the nation's police and secret service. Known as the "sword and the shield of the party," the government agency was so powerful that it reported only to the Socialist Unity Party (SED) headed by Erich Honecker.

There is little doubt that the construction and tacit acceptance of the Berlin Wall, which prevented East Germany's citizens from having normal contact with any other democracies, enabled the Ministry of

State Security to become one of the fundamental instruments of state power. Its foreign intelligence network, headed by the legendary spymaster, Markus Wolf, was so sophisticated that an East German spy, Günter Guillaume, succeeded in being appointed private secretary to West German Chancellor Willy Brandt, an association that caused the latter's downfall in 1974, when Guillaume's political affiliation was uncovered.

However, the Stasi's surveillance of diplomats, journalists, businessmen, and other foreigners represented only a fraction of its activities—its chief business was an obsessive search for political opponents within East Germany itself. Erich Mielke, the Stasi's head, was convinced that every citizen represented a potential security hazard and that it was his obligation to "know everything everywhere."

To achieve this impossible goal, the Stasi eventually employed close to 100,000 full-time employees (all of whom were members of the SED), as well as another 174,000 to work unofficially on its behalf, including between 20,000 and 30,000 secret informers based in West Germany. (Since the Stasi's dismantling, almost 300 West German informers have been tried for their collaboration and admitted to being on the Stasi payroll. One informant confessed to accepting one million DM over a period of five years in exchange for spying.)

"It is hard for anyone who has grown up in a democracy to know what it is like to live in a police state," notes staff volunteer Steffen Leide, who is in charge of giving English-language tours of the museum complex. "Many people don't realize that whereas there was one Gestapo agent

THIS ARCHITECTURAL MODEL OF THE FORMER STASI HEADQUARTERS WAS MADE
BY THE MINISTRY OF STATE SECURITY TO HELP POSITION GUARDS AROUND THE COMPLEX.
AT ONE TIME, THIS AREA WAS THE WORKPLACE FOR BOTH THE DEPARTMENTS
OF COUNTERESPIONAGE, FOREIGN INTELLIGENCE, AND DOMESTIC SPYING.
A CITY WITHIN A CITY, IT HAD A BANK, A HOSPITAL, AND A SHOPPING CENTER.

for every 20,000 Germans, there was one Stasi agent for every two hundred East Germans. In a country of seventeen million citizens, six million had a Stasi file."

In addition to relying on an elaborate network of informers who spied on their neighbors, colleagues, and spouses, the agency bugged houses and eavesdropped on telephone conversations. (In East Berlin alone there were three telephone wiretapping stations, where more than 200 people worked around the clock.)

The Stasi also established a manufacturing unit that specialized in producing elaborate spying devices, some of which are on display in the museum. While none of this equipment was ever featured in a James Bond movie, one is still surprised to see that almost anything could be used for domestic espionage: cameras,

microphones, and other types of bugging devices were hidden in evening bags, camera bags, watering cans, window boxes, gas station canisters (the Stasi controlled all filling stations along the East German border), and even in the doors of the Trabant, the ubiquitous East German car.

Although the Stasi's employees managed to destroy thirty percent of the agency's files, they nonetheless left behind 17,000 plastic bags filled with ripped files (the equivalent of 180 kilometers), which are now being painstakingly pieced together and reviewed. "Two people need a full month to reconstruct a single bag," notes Leide. "There are also Stasi movies, videos, and tape-recordings, and fifty million card files to sort through," he continues. "There are three thousand people working on this project, which we think could

THIS WATERING CAN
WAS OUTFITTED WITH A HIDDEN CAMERA.
SUCH SURVEILLANCE EQUIPMENT WAS USED TO AVOID
RAISING SUSPICIONS
THAT THE STASI MIGHT BE SPYING ON ANYONE AND EVERYONE.

take as long as forty years to complete."

Two highlights of this museum are the starkly appointed personal office and living quarters of Erich Mielke, whose heroes were Karl Marx, Vladimir Ilyich Lenin, and Felix

Mielke then fled to the Soviet Union during the 1930s, where he became a specialist in counterinsurgency and security matters, thus ensuring a senior position for himself in this field upon his return to Germany's Russian-occupied sector in

THIS INNOCUOUS SHOULDER BAG HAD A HIDDEN CAMERA SEWN INSIDE ITS LINING.
EVEN THE PANELS OF CAR DOORS WERE EQUIPPED
WITH INFRARED LIGHTS FOR TAKING PHOTOGRAPHS AT NIGHT.

Dzerzhinsky (the founder of the Cheka, the Soviet Union's precursor to the KGB). Born in 1907 to an impoverished Berlin working-class family, Mielke first gained renown in 1931, by organizing and helping to carry out the assassination of two police captains known for their brutality toward left-wing political demonstrators. (On October 26, 1993, Mielke was sentenced to six years imprisonment for his role in this assassination, but was acquitted of all other charges. Considered too ill to stand trial, Mielke only served two years of his sentence.)

1945. Having helped establish the GDR's Ministry of State Security, first as a branch of the Ministry of the Interior, then as a separate government agency, he served successively as deputy to its first two heads, Wilhelm Zaisser and Ernst Wollweber, both of whom were later purged. After Wollweber's fall, Mielke took over as chief of the Stasi, a position he held until the Ministry's demise in November 1989.

Next to Mielke's office is a small, unassuming room which people believe was once used to instruct prosecutors shortly before important

FIFTEEN STASI DISTRICT LEADERS UNDER ERICH MIELKE'S DIRECT COMMAND
USED TO MEET IN THIS CONFERENCE ROOM.
BEHIND THE CHAIR OCCUPIED BY THE MINISTER OF STATE SECURITY
IS A PAINTING BY WALTER FRANKENSTEIN,
A WELL-KNOWN COMMUNIST ARTIST,
THAT SHOWS YOUNGSTERS STANDING IN FRONT OF THE BERLIN WALL,
EXPRESSING THEIR "THANKS" FOR
THE "ERECTION OF
THE 'ANTI-FASCIST PROTECTION WALL.' "

political trials. Today, a small art gallery has been installed in this room featuring the work of dissident artists, including the artist Sieghard Pohl, who was incarcerated four years for creating art that openly criticized the East German government's policies.

During its heyday, almost anyone could be arrested as long as the Stasi could fabricate a reason under the broad category "crimes against the state," which included speaking out against the government or attempting to escape the country. Between 1961 and 1990, it is estimated that the Ministry of State Security had imprisoned over 200,000 East Germans. The Stasi may go down in history as one of the few government agencies to profit from the sale of its political prisoners: to raise hard currency, the GDR sold nearly 35,000 political prisoners to the West German government for 3.5 billion DM!

Today it is deeply satisfying to see that in this former bastion of terror, where the fate of thousands of people's lives could be determined by the information on a four-by-five file card, or from an overheard conversation, the practices and schemes of the Stasi have not only been unmasked but are now exposed for all to see and judge. This valuable museum holds lessons for everyone, demonstrating what can happen when a totalitarian regime indulges its worst impulses while trying to dominate the lives and even the thoughts of its people.

Peacock Island

Düppel Forest, Berlin
Tel: 805–3042

Open every day except Monday
10:00 A.M. to 1:00 P.M. and
1:30 P.M. to 5:00 P.M.
Mid-May to Mid-October.

S-Bahn: 1 to Wannsee, then Bus
216 to the ferry, which sails
regularly to Peacock Island
The last guided tour offered to
visitors commences a half-hour
prior to closing.

I N 1821, the artist Eduard Lautier was inspired to paint a charming view from the east bank of the Havel River, showing the towers of a castle peeping through the island's wild and overgrown landscape. Seeing this painting, it seems as if this tableau had materialized from a fairy tale, one in which Sleeping Beauty would have felt entirely at home.

Happily, this enchanting perspective does not emanate solely from an artist's imagination, but can be seen today by visiting the Pfaueninsel, a two-hundred-acre historic estate that still boasts an exquisitely appointed castle, beautifully maintained gardens and plantings, as well as ancient trees and abundant bird life. Only thirteen miles from the center of Berlin, and accessible by a five-minute ferry ride, the island retains an unparalleled pastoral aura virtually undisturbed for almost two centuries. But don't be misled by what you see. Peacock Island is a work of art—a felicitous combination of Neoclassical and Neo-Gothic architecture and English-style landscaping.

Known as "the Pearl in the Havel Sea," the island was bequeathed by the Great Elector Friederich Wilhelm (1640–1688), to the renowned chemist Johann Kunckel von Löwenstern, who built a short-lived laboratory on its eastern bank, where precious ruby glass was produced for the court by Andreas Cassius of Lübeck. However, by 1689 the laboratory had burned down, and it was around this time that part of the island was turned over to the Potsdam Orphanage.

By the time the island was

CONSTRUCTED TO RESEMBLE
A NEO-GOTHIC MOCK RUIN,
THE SUMMER PALACE ON PEACOCK ISLAND
IS MADE OF WOOD THAT HAS BEEN
CONCEALED BY "PETRIFICATION,"
A PROCESS THAT CONSISTS OF STREWING SAND
IN THE COAT OF PAINT.

acquired in 1783 by Friedrich Wilhelm II as a romantic hideaway for himself and his mistress, the beautiful Wilhelmine von Encke, daughter of a trumpetist at the court (and whom the king later ennobled as the Countess Lichtenau), it had grown into a wilderness of oak trees, which added to its mystery and romance. Leaving most of the island in its original state, the king camped here with his court beneath Oriental tents, reflecting his era's passion for romantic exoticism. This was borne out even further by the introduction of peacocks, which still have the run of the island and gave it its name.

Weary of living in makeshift tents, in 1794 Friedrich Wilhelm II commissioned the court carpenter, Johann Gottlieb Brendel, to build a summer palace on the western end of the island so that its façade faced visitors arriving by boat from Potsdam. Made to resemble a Neo-Gothic mock ruin, the palace is made of wood, then concealed by "petrification," which consists of strewing sand in the coat of paint. Its two towers (originally connected by a primitive wooden bridge), are joined by a delicate cast-iron bridge, designed in 1807 by the Berlin Iron Foundry, and still in use today. A well-restored trompe-l'oeil landscape mural painted in the arched niche on the main façade gives the impression of an open gateway leading into the

QUEEN LUISE'S BEDROOM WITH ITS WHITE MARBLE FIREPLACE
RETAINS THE ORIGINAL FABRIC WALL-COVERING OF EAST INDIAN CHINTZ.
THE BED, WHICH IS DECORATED WITH CARVED OAK LEAVES,
WAS MADE BY THE SCULPTOR ANGERMANN.

park beyond. Besides building a
kitchen with an ice cellar nearby,
Brendel also constructed a dairy in
the semblance of a ruin, again
emphasizing the triumph of nature
over man.

Unfortunately, the Prussian king
never had time to appreciate his
man-made paradise, since he died of
dropsy in 1797, the same year the
summer palace was completed. His
death caused the downfall of the
Countess Lichtenau, and marked the

end of the court's infatuation with
untamed nature. While the monarch's
successor, Friedrich Wilhelm III,
initially introduced animal husbandry
and crops to the island, farming had
lost its appeal by 1822. Instead,
Germany's foremost gardener, Peter
Joseph Lenné, was commissioned to
alter the surrounding landscape.
Visitors can still admire his splendid
achievement; a stroll on the island
imparts a variety of pastoral pleasures,
be they gazing at long stretches of

woodland, or rambling through a Biedermeier garden, or glimpsing different follies time and again from a favorable vantage point.

A high point in the visit is a guided tour of the castle on the Pfaueninsel. Consisting of four rooms each on the lower and upper floors, it remains essentially unchanged since it was first completed and furnished in 1797. The rich stucco work on the walls and ceilings, the hand-painted ceiling frescoes, the parquet floors of precious woods, and the elegant Neoclassical and Biedermeier furniture, give visitors a vivid sense of the intimate elegance that induced Friedrich Wilhelm III and his spouse, Queen Luise, to make frequent visits to the castle during the summer months.

One room pays tribute to Prussia's beloved and courageous Queen Luise (1776–1810), whose warm nature and passionate espousal of resistance to Napoleon, endeared her to contemporaries and subsequent generations. The careful fostering of the myth of the young and lovely Queen, who died in 1810 as a result of privations suffered during the French occupation of Prussia, is borne out in Johannes Erdmann Hummel's watercolor depicting the exterior and interior view of Luise's renowned Mausoleum in Charlottenburg. Adding to the room's charm and intimacy is a screen pasted with cut-out prints and flower drawings made by the royal couple's children. (Ironically, sixty years later, on the same day Luise died, her youngest son Wilhelm I was declared Emperor of Germany in the Hall of Mirrors at Versailles, following France's defeat in the Franco-Prussian War.)

Perhaps the palace's most unusual room is the turquoise tearoom decorated with twenty-nine allegorical white plaster cast reliefs by Johannes Peter Egtler, whose random mythological motifs convey the impression of a small collection of antiquities. A life-size plaster figure of Pomona, the Goddess of Fruit, made by the Berlin sculptor and stove manufacturer Philipp Rode, underscores the residence's rural character.

This adulation of a natural way of life removed from European civilization, popularized by the philosopher Jean-Jacques Rousseau in the late eighteenth century, is underscored in the circular Otaheite or Tahiti Cabinet in the castle's north tower. Hand-painted murals by Peter Ludwig Lütke give one the sensation of being inside a bamboo hut, despite the presence of a Greek-style ceiling fixture. This room was decorated at a time when both the South Seas *and* Greek antiquity were equated with the ideal of a pure and unspoiled society.

On the upper floor, the gallery, which was once used for dancing and musical soirées, occupies the entire width of the palace. A Neoclassical interior, normally executed in stone or stucco, has been achieved with various types of wood carving and inlay. Only the fireplace and the reliefs above the doors are made of marble. The royal infatuation with the antique is reflected in the Roman-inspired reliefs, which portray such mythical couples as Urania and Socrates, Homer and Clio, Amalthea and the young Jupiter, as well as Thea and Saturn. The ceiling frescoes also evoke ancient Rome: the centerpiece is a copy of Guido Reni's famous *Aurora*, in the Palazzo Rospigliosi, while the two smaller oval frescoes on either side of it were modeled on frescoes by Annibale Carracci.

In keeping with the royal court's predilection for the exotic, parts of the Pfaueninsel were converted into a

THE PLASTER FIGURE OF POMONA, THE
GODDESS OF FRUIT, WAS MADE BY THE
BERLIN STOVE MANUFACTURER AND
SCULPTOR PHILIPP RODE.

THIS PASTEL PORTRAIT OF QUEEN LUISE
BY NIKOLAUS LAUER
SHOWS WHY SHE WAS CELEBRATED
THROUGHOUT EUROPE
FOR BOTH HER CHARM AND BEAUTY.
THE GERMAN ROMANTIC POET
JEAN-PAUL CALLED
HER "THE NOBLE MUSE."

THIS MARBLE RELIEF,
MODELED AFTER AN ANTIQUE ROMAN MODEL,
STANDS OUT LIKE A CAMEO
AGAINST THE CARVED OAK FRAMES ABOVE
THE DOORS IN THE LARGE GALLERY.

zoo in the 1820s, and the island soon became known for its ape and kangaroo house, its stall for wild Chinese pigs, as well as its eagles' cage, bear pit, and llama house. So fascinated was the court by ethnology, that the king invited a native from the Hawaiian Islands to live on the Pfaueninsel. Open to the public twice a week, visitors flocked to the island to admire the animals and the unusual Palm House, designed to resemble an Indian Palace. (Karl Blechen's fanciful paintings of the Palm House are the only extant attestations of that building, which was destroyed in a fire.)

In his 1854 book on *Potsdam's Royal Palaces and Gardens,* August Kopisch wrote: "A visit to the Pfaueninsel was considered the best family outing of the year for the Berlin population. Youngsters took the greatest delight in seeing the monkeys' high-spirited capers, the bears' quaint ungainliness, and the strange skip of the kangaroos.

THE CIRCULAR OTAHEITE CABINET IN
THE NORTH TOWER IS DECORATED WITH
MURALS PAINTED BY PETER LUDWIG
LÜTKE TO CREATE THE IMPRESSION OF
THE INTERIOR OF A BAMBOO HUT.

The tropical plants were admired with many an enraptured ah! One dreamt of being in India and viewed the animal world imported from the south with a mixture of longing and dread."

Friedrich Wilhelm III's death in 1840 marked the end of the Pfaueninsel's era as an exotic paradise, and by 1842 most of the animals had been transferred to the newly established Zoological Garden in Berlin. Yet, even with wild animals no longer the chief attraction, the Pfaueninsel has continued to bewitch visitors from all over the world, including the German writer Theodor Fontane, who described it as "an enigmatic island, an oasis, a carpet of flowers in the Mark." It's in this unspoiled oasis that one can find not only a respite from contemporary urban life, but also the setting for a variety of aesthetic and pastoral pleasures unique to this part of Germany.

Prince Pückler Museum-Branitz Castle and Park

Zum Kavalierhaus 11
03042 Cottbus
Tel: (03–55) 75–12–21

Open Tuesday through Sunday
10:00 A.M. to Noon and 12:30 P.M.
to 5:00 P.M.
November to March
Open Tuesday through Sunday
10:00 A.M. to Noon and 12:30 P.M.
to 6:00 P.M.
April to October

By train: Take the train from
Lichtenberg Station in Berlin to
Cottbus; then take the 15 bus to
Branitz Park and the Fürst Pückler
Museum.

Restaurant on premises.

ALTHOUGH the three Egyptian pyramids at Giza from the Fourth Dynasty (2680–2565 B.C.) are world-renowned, few people are aware that they served as models for two extraordinary earth pyramids in Branitz Park, a magnificent 237–acre estate on the southeastern outskirts of the industrial city of Cottbus, which was conceived by Germany's great eccentric of garden design, Prince Hermann Ludwig Heinrich Pückler-Muskau (1785–1871).

Pückler—who never did anything by halves—left instructions that, upon his death, his body should be placed in a boat and rowed across the park's man-made lake ("the River of the Underworld") to a sixty-foot-high

TO CREATE THE SPLENDID BRANITZ CASTLE AND PARK,
PRINCE PÜCKLER DIRECTED PRISONERS FROM THE TOWN TO TRANSFORM THE FLAT PLAIN
INTO A SERIES OF HILLS AND WINDING PATHS,
SET OFF BY MAN-MADE LAKES, FLOWING STREAMS, AND BRIDGED-OVER PONDS.

THIS ELEGANT PERGOLA, SET OFF BY A REPLICA OF THE *VENUS OF CAPUA* BY ANTONIO CANOVA, FACES THE MAIN HOUSE, WHICH WAS BUILT BY PÜCKLER'S GRANDFATHER.

sepulchral pyramid *(Tumulus);* there his body would be safely interred for eternity. Unfortunately, his carefully prepared scheme did not go exactly as planned. When he died in February 1871, the lake was frozen over, so his servants had no choice but to carry their master's coffin across a temporary bridge to the pyramid.

When it came to gardening, Pückler's aims were almost as grandiose as those of the pharaohs. To create his English-style park, he spent the equivalent of a king's ransom, buying up huge parcels of land, including the entire village of Branitz. Working with prisoners from Cottbus, he directed them to transform the flat plain into a series of hills, winding paths, and sepulchral mounds, and to set them off with man-made lakes, flowing streams, and bridged-over ponds. The park was then planted with oak, lime, copper beech, and hornbeam, as well as

robinia, chestnut, spruce, ash, and maple trees.

In accordance with his concept of extending his living-space into the outdoors, Pückler designed a lavish pergola decorated with sixteen terra-cotta reliefs whose antique motifs were based on sketches by the Danish Neoclassical sculptor Bertel Thorwaldsen. To complete the overall effect of enchantment, he created a blue-painted, wrought-iron, vine-covered outdoor rotunda that high-lights the gold-plated bust of the famous German soprano Henriette Sontag and dotted the park with other statues, including two Neoclassical sculptures, the *Venus of Italica* by Thorwaldsen and the *Venus of Capua* by Antonio Canova.

"Branitz Park is Pückler's last great work of art," notes Matthias Körner, the museum's director of public relations. "He was not only the first landscape designer to put earth pyramids in a park, he was the first one to show that there was no need to separate the ornamental part of the garden with its statues and flower beds from the fields and hills beyond," he adds. "He wanted visitors to be able to stand anywhere in this park and see the natural equivalent of a harmonious landscape painting." Beautifully restored to its original grandeur, the park lives up to Pückler's ambitions, providing the visiting ambler with an endless number of entrancing vistas to gaze upon.

However, a day spent at the Baroque Branitz Castle (the nobleman's ancestral home) would certainly be incomplete without visiting the handsomely appointed museum that documents Pückler's adventurous life, which was devoted to women, writing, and globe-trotting—as well as gardening. His dashing demeanor and consummate charm were to serve him

THIS *VENUS OF ITALICA* SCULPTURE
BY THE DANISH NEOCLASSICAL
SCULPTOR, BERTEL THORWALDSEN,
IS PAINTED IN FLESH TONES
AND DRESSED IN VIVID BLUE DRAPERY.

well, considering his inauspicious beginnings. Not only did his father dissipate his own family's inheritance, but he also seriously depleted his wife's estate. After reading law for a few semesters and trying his luck in the army, Pückler traveled to London in search of a wealthy bride to restore his family's fortune. During his two-year stay, he visited many country estates designed by Capability Brown and Sir Humphrey Repton. While the Prince failed to find a suitable match, he returned to Germany afflicted with what he called *parkomanie.*

In 1817, he met and married a wealthy divorcée, Countess Lucie von Pappenheim, daughter of Prince Karl August von Hardenberg, the Chancellor of Prussia. Furnished with both an ample dowry and an unfettered imagination, Pückler spent the next three decades redesigning his entire 1,853-acre principality, turning it into a Reptonesque version of the English landscaped park. However, his dream project at Muskau came to a grinding halt when the couple ran out of money. The pragmatic Lucie suggested they get a divorce so the Prince could find another rich woman to finance his park. After their pro forma divorce (on the grounds that they could not produce an heir), Lucie continued to reside at Muskau, while Pückler returned to England in 1826 to find a suitable new wife.

During his second sojourn in London, Pückler took along his head gardener to show him the English landscaping ideas he wished to have incorporated on his Muskau estate. Together, they visited Regent's Park, Kew, Hampton Court, Chiswick House, Blenheim Palace, Woburn, Tintern Abbey, Kenwood, and Warwick Castle's gardens. The impressions gathered during this tour would later be distilled in Pückler's 1834 work *Hints on Landscape*

PÜCKLER'S MAGNIFICENT LIBRARY IS DOMINATED BY HIS MARBLE BUST AND A GIGANTIC BAROQUE BRASS CHANDELIER OF HIS OWN DESIGN.

Gardening. Through the "controlling scheme" he applied toward the outdoors, his aim was to extoll "untrammeled Nature, where the hand of man is visible only in the well-kept roads and judiciously scattered buildings." Among his revolutionary precepts was suggesting that parks provide both educational and therapeutic benefits for the public—a viewpoint which was to inspire many city parks built during the nineteenth century. Pückler's advice on landscaping became widely sought after, even by the French Emperor Napoleon III, who requested his assistance with the redesign of Paris's Bois de Boulogne. Although the German prince had no actual hand in the park's improvements, his writings and work at Muskau influenced the park's subsequent Anglicization.

When Pückler wasn't busy with new landscaping schemes, he was actively courting an endless stream of women. "He was one of the most famous dandies of his time," notes Körner. "It is said he had more lovers than Casanova and Don Juan combined. He wrote hundreds of letters, often starting each one, 'You're the only one I've ever loved.' After his death, they found a note attached to a pack of love letters, which read 'To be used again, if necessary.' "

Once, when he wished to attract the attention of a woman in Berlin, he rode down Unter den Linden to the Café Kranzler in a carriage drawn by white reindeer—an incident that was later immortalized in an illustrated periodical. The one young woman who marked his life profoundly was a strikingly beautiful Ethiopian princess, named Machbuba, whom he purchased at a Cairo slave market in 1837, while he was the guest of the Viceroy of Egypt. Although the exotic, turbaned princess attracted much attention when Pückler traveled with her to Vienna, her European sojourn proved miserable and short-lived—within a few months after her arrival at Muskau, she fell ill with fever and died while the Prince was away in Berlin. "Pückler always regretted having abandoned her," notes Körner, pointing to the plaster casts of Machbuba's head and hands that were made after the young girl's death, and which are now displayed in a Moorish-style room in a glass case beneath her portrait.

While Pückler failed to find an heiress in England, he discovered something almost as lucrative—literary inspiration. His lively letters to Lucie, which were filled with vivid, and often amusing accounts of his travels, and which captured such disparate personalities as Sir Walter Scott, Beau Brummel, and Charles

THIS ELABORATE WHITE BAROQUE CERAMIC STOVE
DOMINATES THE CONCERT HALL WHERE AFTERNOON RECITALS ARE STILL HELD.

THIS LAKE PYRAMID, WHICH WAS CONSTRUCTED AS A GRAVE SITE FOR PÜCKLER AND HIS WIFE, LUCIE, WAS INSPIRED BY THE PYRAMIDS AT GIZA IN EGYPT.

Dickens, were eventually published in a four-volume unsigned work *Briefe eines Verstorbenen (Letters of a Dead Man,* renamed *The Tour of A German Prince,* in the English translation of 1832). Translated into half a dozen languages, the book became a sensation all over the Continent and in the United States. It was even hailed by Goethe, who wrote that Pückler's letters "belong to the highest class of literature."

Although the royalties from *Letters of a Dead Man* brought in some money, they were never enough to cover the couple's extravagant expenses. Eventually, they were forced to sell Muskau and move to Pückler's family estate in Branitz. Although the couple never remarried, they lived together until Lucie's death in 1854. A tour of the eclectically decorated and furnished Castle Branitz reveals a curious composite of garishly painted *boiseries,* bombastic Neo-Renaissance furnishings, overblown light fixtures, kitsch paintings, and rare antiquities,

including four ancient Egyptian canopic burial jars Pückler brought back from his travels. Here, miles away from the capital, the bon vivant prince entertained the leading luminaries of his day, including the Crown Prince (the future Emperor William I) and Bismarck. Oblivious of public opinion, he lived exactly as he pleased, often receiving his guests in Oriental garb, complete with turban and flowing robes.

It seems that nothing was too outlandish for this singular personality— he even allowed a local ice-cream maker to use his name. To this day, Germans are more familiar with Pückler ice-cream (similar to the Italian *spumoni*) than with the Prince's literary or horticultural achievements. Now, thanks to the splendid restoration of Branitz Park and Castle, visitors can explore the multifaceted beauty of this unusual showplace, and learn more about the life and times of the intriguing and free-spirited man who created it.

Schloss Rheinsberg

Rheinsberg Castle

16831 Rheinsberg
Tel: (0339) 31–21–05

Open Tuesday through Saturday
9:30 A.M. to 12:30 P.M. and
1:00 P.M. to 4:45 P.M.

By train: Take the train from
Lichtenberg Station to Rheinsberg,
then take a taxi to the castle.

ALTHOUGH Frederick the Great (1712–1786) lived at Rheinsberg Castle for only four years, he was later to confess: "I have always been dogged with bad luck; the only place where I was happy was Rheinsberg." Knowing his troubled relations with his father, Friedrich Wilhelm I ("the Soldier King"), his chronic ill health, and the devastation inflicted upon his kingdom as a result of the Seven Years' War (1756–1763), one can understand why the aged Prussian monarch would recall with nostalgia his youthful idyll on this estate overlooking Grienerick Lake.

Fortuitously located eighty kilometers north of Berlin, Rheinsberg

THIS VIEW OF RHEINSBERG CASTLE
IN WINTER REVEALS
A WOODEN DRAWBRIDGE OVER A DRY MOAT
THAT IS NORMALLY HIDDEN BY TREES.

Castle was a delightful oasis away from his father's rough and spartan court, which Frederick openly scorned. Whereas the crown prince was an ardent admirer of Gallic culture, as well as an accomplished flutist and composer, the king loathed everything that was French; moreover, his favorite pastime was the *tapagie*, an all-male debauch of smoking and drinking.

The hostility the king bore towards Frederick changed overnight to hatred, upon learning that his son was plotting to flee to England with an officer, Hans Hermann von Katte. Betrayed at the last minute and imprisoned by his father in the fortress of Küstrin, Frederick was forced to witness his friend Katte's execution. Had the Habsburg Emperor Charles VI not interceded on his behalf, Frederick might have suffered the same fate.

Only after the Crown Prince reluctantly agreed to wed the German Princess Elizabeth-Christine of Brunswick, did his father release him from prison. Realizing that Frederick and his new bride needed a suitable residence, the king purchased the estate at Rheinsberg, and commissioned Johann Gottfried Kemmeter, his Superintendent of Building Works, to convert the old sixteenth-century castle complex (which included a gatehouse, brewery, and main wing with a round tower) into a handsome Baroque edifice.

While Kemmeter tore down the brewery, filled in the moat, and built a north wing, Rheinsberg's present appearance reflects the concepts of the architect and painter Georg Wenzeslaus von Knobelsdorff, who took over the castle's reconstruction upon his return from Italy in 1737. (After demonstrating his exceptional

PRINCESS AMELIA'S RED ROOM IS COVERED IN RED DAMASK
WITH A FREDERICIAN RIBBON PATTERN. THE LARGE ANTOINE PESNE PORTRAIT
OVER THE TAPESTRY-COVERED SOFA IS OF PRINCE LEOPOLD
OF ANHALT-DESSAU, THE INVENTOR OF THE SO-CALLED MILITARY "GOOSE-STEP."

PRINCESS AMELIA'S APARTMENTS WITH DOORS IN *ENFILADE* WERE REMODELED TO SHOW
THE INFLUENCE OF FRENCH DECOR: WHITE AND GOLD *BOISERIES*, DECORATIVE MOLDINGS,
AND ELABORATELY FRAMED MIRRORS SET INTO THE WALL.

THE WALLS OF PRINCE HENRY'S SHELL ROOM ARE MADE OF GREEN AND YELLOW MARBLED
STUCCO, AND SET OFF WITH STUCCO CHERUB RELIEFS, THAT ARE FESTOONED WITH REAL
SHELLS AND CORAL—AN UNUSUAL HOMAGE TO THE ROCAILLE PERIOD.

talent at Rheinsberg, Knobelsdorff later designed Frederick's palace at Sanssouci.)

Constrained by Kemmeter's design and a limited budget (Frederick was often so short of funds, that he had to borrow money to buy books), Knobelsdorff can only be credited with the projection of the castle's central wing and the final design of the inner courtyard's colonnade connecting the two lateral wings. The finished edifice is an elegant three-winged Baroque building, whose central wing is reached via a wooden bridge. Above the entrance is a cartouche with the Latin inscription: *Friderico Tranquillitatem Colenti. MDCCXXXIX* ("Frederick's [house], who cultivates serenity.1739.")

In her biography, *Frederick the Great*, Nancy Mitford describes how the prince led a full life at Rheinsberg, reading between six and seven hours a day to acquire a solid grounding in European literature and philosophy. It was during this brief and peaceful interval that he prepared to rule Prussia. "Good intentions, love of mankind, and the hard work of a solitary can perhaps be beneficial to society and I flatter myself that I am not among its idle, useless members," he wrote to one of his father's friends.

At Rheinsberg, he began his famous correspondence with Voltaire (which would last until the French philosopher's death), and commenced his own prolific literary output. He also found time to compose music, including the opera *Montezuma*. In the evening he entertained his small coterie of friends (which never exceeded twenty people), by putting on a concert or a play, which was generally written either by Racine or Voltaire.

It was also at this time that he began his collection of French Rococo painters: Antoine Watteau (1684–1721) and his pupils: Nicolas Lancret (1690–1745) and Jean-Baptiste Pater (1695–1736). Like the refined and cultured French monarchs he so wished to emulate, he surrounded himself with numerous artists, including the stucco-worker Johann Carl Scheffler, the portraitist and historical painter Antoine Pesne, and the landscape painter Auguste Dubuisson. Under Knobelsdorff's direction, they collaborated on transforming Rheinsberg into an entrancing work of art evoked in *Les Fêtes Galantes* of Watteau, Boucher, and Fragonard.

After Frederick became king, he bequeathed Rheinsberg to his brother Henry, taking only his furniture and paintings to Potsdam. From 1752 to 1802, when the castle was Prince Henry's primary residence, Georg Friedrich Boumann the Younger was commissioned to build an outdoor theater and a Cavaliers' House to lodge the prince's courtiers. (The theater, which suffered damage during World War II, is being restored with funds from the European Community.)

By the time Henry died in 1802, Rheinsberg's heyday was past. From 1843 onward, the estate was governed by the royal exchequer until the fall of Kaiser Wilhelm II. Although spared wartime bombing, the castle was looted after 1945, and consequently some of its built-in mirrors, overdoor panels, and mantelpieces were destroyed. In 1953 the Social Security office transformed the palace, stables, and other outbuildings into East Germany's first sanatorium for diabetics, which remained open until 1990. A display of photographs illustrates the incongruity of installing such medical facilities inside the castle. Seeing gilded *boiseries* supporting washstands, a painting gallery transformed into an examining-room,

THIS AIRY STAIRCASE
WITH ITS PLAIN UNFINISHED WOODEN PLANK FLOORING
AND ITS INVITING CHERUBIM
DEMONSTRATE THE SIMPLICITY AND CHARM
OF THE COUNTRY ESTATE
FREDERICK LOVED SO MUCH.

and a Neoclassical library turned into a commissary-kitchen, one might conclude that the needs of patients took precedence over any other considerations.

It seems that the decision to install the sanatorium at Rheinsberg was as much political as practical. "Between the 1950s and the 1980s, Prussian history, including that of Frederick the Great, was viewed as imperialistic, militaristic, and reactionary—anything that glorified it had to be repudiated," explains Dr. Detlef Fuchs, the castle's castellan, and a former East German

national. "There was also the feeling that it was about time the people benefited from palaces once reserved only for kings."

Since the reunification of Germany and the transfer of the Rheinsberg estate to the Berlin-Brandenburg Prussian Palaces and Gardens Foundation in 1995, the castle and grounds have been transformed into a public museum, with twenty of its rooms open to the public. Slowly, painstakingly, the palace is regaining its former splendor, thanks to a diligent and talented team of restorers. Today, visitors can discover the earliest Frederician interiors decorated by Knobelsdorff, such as Frederick's former Library and the Hall of Mirrors, decorated with gilded doorways, marbled stucco walls, and Antoine Pesne's luscious ceiling painting *Aurora, Goddess of Dawn, Floats Before the Sun Chariot of Apollo, while the Goddess of Night Flees,* reputedly a sardonic allegory on Frederick the Great's coronation.

The apartments of Prince Henry's sister, Princess Amelia, remodeled for her visit in 1762, demonstrate the evolution of Frederician rococo. The Red Room, notable for its gilded stucco ceiling rosette and red silk damask-covered walls, features a collection of portraits revealing Prince Henry's social and military ties, as well as his connections with the French court. (During the French Revolution, Rheinsberg became a haven for the French aristocracy.)

Prince Henry's predilection for *rocaille* is evident in the splendid Shell Room (designed by Carl Gotthard Langhans), with its elaborate gilded stucco ceiling, ornamented with coral and seashells. His later penchant for the Neoclassical is demonstrated in his columned Library, where the ceiling is painted with signs of the Zodiac and twenty-two portraits of classical poets and scholars.

Since the castle is also inextricably linked with Kurt Tucholsky's charming novella *Rheinsberg—A Picture Book for Lovers,* it now houses a small museum devoted to the German writer, best remembered for his biting satire directed at Germany's militarism and nationalism. Although the Jewish-born Tucholsky emigrated to Sweden in 1924, he was stripped of his citizenship in 1933, the same year his books were banned by the Nazis. Two years later, he committed suicide.

The artistic heritage of Rheinsberg is being revived with an annual international opera festival that encourages the work of young, undiscovered talent. In addition, some of the palace's rooms have been set aside for temporary exhibitions of avant-garde painting and sculpture. In keeping with its lengthy literary heritage, Rheinsberg also sponsors monthly readings of contemporary German authors. "When Frederick lived at Rheinsberg, all the arts flourished," notes Dr. Fuchs. "This is where the young Langhans, the young Knobelsdorff, even the young Tucholsky, did their first masterpieces. Our hope is to resurrect that creative spirit." If Frederick were in residence at Rheinsberg today, it's more than likely he would be the first to endorse this creative aspiration.

THIS PORTRAIT OF THE "SOLDIER KING,"
FREDERICK'S IRASCIBLE MILITARIST FATHER,
REPRESENTS AN IMPOSING PRESENCE
IN THE HALL OF MIRRORS.

Schinkel Pavilion

Luisenplatz
14059 Berlin
Tel: 32091–212

Open Tuesday through Friday
9:00 A.M. to 5:00 P.M.
Saturdays and Sundays
10:00 A.M. to 5:00 P.M.

U-Bahn: Richard Wagner Platz
Bus: 109, 110, 145, X21, X26

SCHINKEL'S DESIGN FOR
THE NEW PAVILION
INCORPORATES A NUMBER OF
FEATURES FROM THE VILLA REALE,
A NEOPOLITAN PALACE
THAT HAD ENCHANTED HIS PATRON,
FRIEDRICH WILHELM III.
(PHOTO: STIFTUNG PREUSSISCHE
SCHLÖSSER UND
GÄRTEN BERLIN-BRANDENBURG,
SCHLOSS CHARLOTTENBURG, FOTOTHEK)

IN 1825, a year after his morganatic second marriage to the twenty-seven-year-old Duchess von Liegnitz, Friederich Wilhelm III commissioned a small summer residence on the eastern side of the palace grounds at Charlottenburg, almost at the foot of the River Spree. The king desired a simple, elegant private dwelling for his bride and immediate family, with an architectural style that would offer closer contact with light and nature, as opposed to the Baroque palace's burdensome pomp and ostentation. In accordance with his wishes, the building was modeled after the Villa Reale Chiatamone, where the king had stayed during his visit to Naples in 1822.

To bring his project to fruition, he commissioned the court architect who had designed the bedroom and the mausoleum for his first wife, Queen Luise: Karl Friedrich Schinkel (1781–1841), senior councillor for Prussian building activities. This was the man who, within the span of twenty-five years, designed more edifices and structures in Berlin and its outskirts than would most architects in several lifetimes.

Obsessed with work and driven by the conviction that he could improve society through the ideals of architecture, Schinkel's achievements included bridges, gates, schools, churches, palaces, and manor houses—all reflecting his two lifelong sources of inspiration, the architecture of classical Greece and Italy, and Medieval Gothic. No single architect did more to shape the appearance of Berlin than Schinkel, to such an extent that his singular vision remains visible in the city and its outlying areas, notwithstanding the destruction of two world wars. Among his major works are Berlin's first public museum, Altes Museum (The Old Museum), the Schauspielhaus (Playhouse) on the Gendarmenmarkt, the Neue Wache on Unter den Linden (a small guardhouse, shaped like a Roman fort, it has been a war memorial since 1919), the Friedrich Werder Church, and the now

the features the king described about the Villa Reale, without ever having seen the Neapolitan palace. The rigorous geometric order Schinkel conceived for the Neue Wache was also applied to this two-story summer residence, which is built more or less on a square base, a mere fifty-four by fifty-nine feet in area. The white cubic structure, whose austere lines are softened by the surrounding foliage during the summer, is set off by severe moldings, soft-green shut-

THE FOCAL POINT IN THE GROUND-FLOOR GARDEN ROOM
IS A SEMI-CIRCULAR BANQUETTE,
INSPIRED BY THE FAMOUS SEMI-CIRCULAR BENCH AT THE *TOMB OF MAMMIA* IN POMPEII.

destroyed Bauakademie (Academy of Architecture), where he lived and taught.

It is a tribute to this architect's talents that, in his design for this summer home (formerly called the New Pavilion, it is better known today as the Schinkel Pavilion), he was able to incorporate a number of

ters, and a delicate wrought-iron wraparound balcony, whose undersides are painted with gold suns on a blue background.

The king's suggestion concerning the continous balcony, a feature adopted from the Villa Reale, matched Schinkel's own admiration for the houses in the Italian country-

SCHINKEL DESIGNED THIS CIRCULAR KPM TABLE
DEPICTING MONUMENTS AND CASTLES IN AND AROUND BERLIN,
MANY OF WHICH WERE BASED ON THE ARCHITECT'S PLANS.

side, in particular those he had sketched on Sicily and Capri in 1803–1804. Their exterior stairs, habitable roofs, and covered trellises blurred the distinction between life inside the stucco dwellings and the verdant Italian countryside. Even in this comparatively simple pavilion, we can see his insistence on integrating architecture with the surrounding landscape, as well as his desire to follow "in the path of nature, faithfully adhering to her laws, and eschewing arbitrariness."

Simplicity and symmetry also prevail inside the pavilion, with the square floor plan divided neatly into nine similar rooms. Surprisingly modest in scale, none of the rooms have the grandeur or aspirations of Frederick the Great's French-inspired Sanssouci, but instead reflect the cozy intimacy of a bourgeois Biedermeier

interior. Most of them are oriented toward the garden and the River Spree, except for the skylit entrance hall.

Schinkel was responsible not only for the building itself, but for the interior decoration and many of the furnishings, as well. The decor was kept deliberately simple: most of the rooms had only single-color wallpaper in red, yellow, green, blue, or white, with a patterned stenciled border, while the window curtains were all white. Only the walls leading up the stairwell were painted with Julius Schoppe's elaborate Pompeian-style grotesques.

In the ground-floor *Gartensaal* (Garden-Room), which faces west, and is twice the size of any other room in the pavilion, the walls are decorated with imitation gray-green marble made of polished stucco, set off by wood moldings and cornices—an aesthetic choice that unites elegance with economy. Here, the architect's rectilinear order was abandoned in favor of a Pompeian banquette, inspired by the famous *stibadium* (semicircular bench) at the *Tomb of Mammia* in Pompeii that would later serve as model for the Humboldt grave site at Tegel. The bench is upholstered in blue silk rep, and the niche is lined with blue rep embroidered with yellow stars. The blue-and-white banquette was intended for conversation, and for taking tea while viewing the palace and its gardens. The whole setting was highlighted by a small circular tea table Schinkel had designed with an inlaid porcelain top depicting several of his recently completed Berlin great works, including the Altes Museum, the Friedrich Werder Church, Schloss Charlottenhof, Schloss Kleinglienicke, and the Neue Wache.

The architect also furnished the other rooms with carefully selected furnishings and other artifacts, many of which were made to his own design. Schinkel believed it was important to create buildings that reflected an all-encompassing vision, which he referred to as *Gesamtkunstwerk*. Working closely with Peter Beuth (1781–1853), head of the Institute of Trades (who later became a major force in Prussian industry), he encouraged the development of decorative arts in Berlin. Moreover, because he had traveled widely in Great Britain, and had been singularly impressed by its nascent Industrial Revolution, he sketched hundreds of designs for Prussia's iron works and other foundries, as well as for glassware, fabrics, ceramics, and other handicrafts.

Both elegant and simple, Schinkel's designs were among the first to be commercially produced in Germany, earning him the reputation as a precursor in the field of industrial design. (He even designed the famous Iron Cross, the highest honor that could be bestowed on the Prussian military, beginning in 1813 during the Wars of Liberation against Napoleon.)

During the Third Reich, the New Pavilion was splendidly restored to its

THE WALLS LEADING UP THE STAIRWELL ARE ENHANCED BY JULIUS SCHOPPE'S ELABORATE POMPEIAN-STYLE GROTESQUES.

original glory on the occasion of the 1936 Olympics. It is a pity that visitors will never see it as it was then—on November 23, 1943, the summer residence was bombed and its contents burned, including numerous paintings by Schinkel. Almost nothing remained except the outer walls and a few fragments of interior decoration. During the rebuilding process, which lasted from 1957 until 1970, the edifice and most of the interior fixtures were restored, largely with the aid of period photographs and pen, ink, and watercolor drawings of the New Pavilion executed by the architect's associate Albrecht Dietrich Schadow in 1824–25. While the house contains almost none of the original movable items, these were replaced wherever possible by comparable pieces from Schinkel's era, many of which the architect had designed.

THIS ELEGANT CANDELABRA
WITH ITS CARYATID BASE IS ALSO
A SCHINKEL DESIGN;
IT STANDS OUT DRAMATICALLY AGAINST
THE IMITATION GRAY-GREEN
MARBLE MADE OF
POLISHED STUCCO IN THE GARDEN ROOM.

The pavilion's current furnishings comprise a rich collection of decorative arts, including a few wooden chairs with wrought-iron inlay designed by Schinkel, a collection of lacy antique iron jewelry worn by fashionable Berliners during the Wars of Liberation against Napoleon, and pieces from the Iron Cross service from the Berlin Porcelain Manufactory that Friedrich Wilhelm III gave to his field marshals in appreciation of their valiance on the battlefield. Also on display throughout the residence are a number of Neoclassical busts and sculptures by Christian Daniel Rauch (1777–1857) and Johann Gottfried Schadow (1764–1850), depicting different members of the royal family.

Not to be overlooked is an outstanding collection of period drawings, engravings, and topographical paintings by artists from the German Romantic school, including an imaginary landscape linking the Alps to the sea by Caspar David Friedrich (a metaphorical plea for German unity and patriotism), two charming versions of the Palm House on Peacock Island, executed by Carl Blechen (1795–1840), and a painting of an imaginary Gothic cathedral, which Schinkel envisioned to commemorate the fallen heroes in the Wars of Liberation against Napoleon.

The museum's most notable works are a fitting tribute to the man who designed the New Pavilion, while converting Berlin's topography: two impressively painted city panoramas by Eduard Gaertner (1801–1877), which taken together provide a complete overview of Schinkel's buildings from the roof of the Friedrich Werder Church, including edifices which have disappeared from the city's skyline, such as the Neue Packhof (The New Customs-House) and the Bauakademie.

THE PAINTED FIREPLACE MANTEL
AND SIMPLE SCHINKEL CHAIR
ARE HANDSOMELY SET OFF BY THE
YELLOW OCHRE WALLS.
THE PATTERNED STENCILED BORDER
ABOVE THE BASEBOARD
IS ALSO A SCHINKEL INNOVATION.

Perhaps one reason why this elegant pavilion remains unique among Berlin's museums is that it permits the visitor to discover a surprisingly intimate royal residence, while appreciating the diverse and impressive achievements of Prussia's greatest nineteenth-century architect. It seems only fitting that the New Pavilion is now known as the Schinkel Pavilion, in homage to the man who beautified Berlin and helped to make it one of Europe's leading capitals.

Stiftung "Neue Synagoge Berlin-Centrum Judaicum"

The New Synagogue Museum-
The Jewish Center

Oranienburger Strasse 28
10117 Berlin
Tel: 28–44–01316

Open Sunday through Thursday
10:00 A.M. to 5:30 P.M.
Friday from 10:00 A.M. to
1:30 P.M.
Guided tours in English, French,
and Hebrew by prior arrangement.

S-Bahn: 1 to Oranienburger Strasse
Tram: 1, 3
Bus: 157

WHILE many Berliners know that the Nazis desecrated and vandalized the interior of Germany's largest Jewish House of God during the infamous *Kristallnacht* (November 9–10, 1938), few of them are aware that at least one municipal police officer objected to their actions and stopped them from carrying out further destruction.

Upon being informed of the rampage, Wilhelm Krützfeld, an officer at the Hackescher Markt precinct, rushed to the synagogue and forced the SA to leave at gunpoint. He also alerted the fire brigade to extinguish the flames—a highly unusual act, since everywhere else in Germany fire brigades had been ordered not to intervene. As a result of Krützfeld's action, the synagogue was in use again in April 1939. Although he was ordered to appear before the Chief of Police, Krützfeld was not particularly castigated for his actions. In 1992, to commemorate his remarkable courage, the Berlin Senate honored him with a memorial tomb.

This is just one of the numerous little-known events and personalities that have been rescued from oblivion and now figure in a stunning permanent exhibition in the reconstructed New Synagogue in the heart of Old Berlin, a stone's throw from the city's oldest Jewish cemetery, which was destroyed by the Nazis in 1943. Titled " 'Open Ye The Gates' The New Synagogue 1866–1999," this exhibition traces the history of the synagogue and the Jewish life related

THE SPLENDIDLY RESTORED GOLD DOME OF THE NEW SYNAGOGUE MUSEUM,
MORE THAN FIFTY METERS HIGH AND COVERED WITH GILDED BUTTRESSES,
STANDS OUT AGAINST THE SKYLINE OF BERLIN.
ONE OF THE CITY'S MOST STRIKING SIGHTS, IT HAS OFTEN BEEN COMPARED
TO THE ALHAMBRA IN GRANADA.

to it—no small task, knowing how few buildings and records were spared the devastation of World War II.

Even with its elegant presentation, which is enhanced by Frank Fiedler's subtle and mysterious music, the exhibition does not downplay the destruction of the New Synagogue nor of the community surrounding it. After services came to an end in March 1940, the house of worship was confiscated by the *Wehrmacht,* and converted into a warehouse for leather and textile goods. During the war, the building's roof and interior were heavily damaged by bombs. By 1958, the East German Jewish community, reduced to less than 200 members, elected to demolish the main synagogue. Only those parts of the building facing the street would be preserved "for the

purpose of lasting remembrance and as a warning for all times."

It seemed inconceivable in a divided Berlin whose total Jewish population had dwindled to 7,000 (compared to 160,000 before the war), that one could sustain a cultural center honoring the city's Jewish heritage, much less a major synagogue. It wasn't until 1988, on the fiftieth anniversary of *Kristallnacht,* that Erich Honecker, the former Chancellor of the German Democratic Republic, and Edgar Bronfman, President of the World Jewish Congress, agreed to establish the Foundation "New Synagoge Berlin-Centrum Judaicum." Its stated mission was the "reconstruction of the New Synagogue in Oranienburger Strasse as a permanent memorial for present and future generations, to create a center for the fostering and preservation of Jewish culture." With the symbolic laying of the foundation stone in November 1988, the reconstruction of the ruined edifice began. It would take another seven years of reconstruction before the building was reopened on May 7th, 1995, a half century after Germany's surrender in World War II.

Knowing how little remained of the original edifice, it is altogether astonishing that the Foundation was able to reconstruct the remaining historical structure, including its splendid gilded dome, and recover architectural fragments and parts of the interior decoration, which now constitute a major part of the exhibition. They demonstrate both the building's impressive architecture, as well as the violence to which it had been subjected. In the dramatically lit exhibition area, shattered stone capitals, largely obliterated ceiling frescoes, a twisted wrought-iron

torchère, and marble fragments that once constituted the Rabbi's pulpit in front of the Torah Ark, suggest a motley collection of ancient ruins. Still, knowing the modern circumstances that produced such "ruins," it is difficult to view them with the same detachment with which one might view the remnants of another, earlier civilization.

The immensity of the main synagogue, which was intended to accommodate up to 3,200 congregants, can be appreciated by walking across the courtyard behind the building's restored areas. The outline of the former main synagogue is laid out in stone in this open courtyard, providing an indication of what was destroyed. "The concept behind the conservation was to retain as many original parts of the building as possible," explains Dr. Chana C. Schütz, the museum's curator. "What was lost was replaced. The newly refashioned elements were made distinctly visible

THIS SCALE MODEL REPLICATES THE ACTUAL DIMENSIONS OF THE ORIGINAL NEW SYNAGOGUE, BEFORE IT WAS DESTROYED. THE JEWISH CENTER'S RESTORED EDIFICE IS ONLY A FRACTION OF THE FORMER BUILDING.

A HAUNTING PHOTOGRAPH OF THE NEW SYNAGOGUE'S FORMER CONGREGANTS,
TAKEN IN THE 1930S, IS A FOCAL POINT OF THE EXHIBIT.

as such. The decoration of the inner rooms was only restored in those areas where the original design was left. Our aim was to show people they were visiting a building where you could still see the scars of history."

When the New Synagogue was first consecrated on September 5, 1866, in the presence of Germany's Chancellor Otto von Bismarck, it was internationally lauded for its technical and engineering achievements. Its dome, more than fifty meters high and covered with gilded buttresses, stood out against the skyline of central Berlin, reflecting the Jewish community's vitality and pride. Designed by the architect Eduard Knoblauch (1801–1865), it was soon one of the city's most striking sights, prompting one newspaper reporter to write: "Its ornamentation reminds one of the magical rooms of the Alhambra and the most beautiful monuments of Arabian architecture."

The analogy was apt, since the four-teenth-century Alhambra in Granada had inspired Knoblauch's design.

The Moorish-style architecture and magnificent façade also drew criticism from anti-Semites, who charged that the edifice expressed Jewish domination and alienation. Yet the New Synagogue's services, which were based on Reform Judaism, incorporated choral singing and organ music, thus reflecting the Berlin Jewish community's desire to adopt practices characteristic of the Christian liturgy.

The forward-thinking congregation also welcomed the first and only female rabbi in Germany, Regina Jonas (1902–1944), whose photograph is included in the exhibition. After studying at Berlin's Academy for Jewish Studies, she was ordained in 1935. While she was invited to participate in Sabbath services, she was never allowed to preach from the pulpit. Deported to the Theresienstadt concentration camp in November 1942, she was killed in Auschwitz in October 1944.

Through period photographs and explanatory texts, visitors can learn more about the activities of numerous Jewish businesses and social services that addressed the needs of immigrants, many of whom were fleeing the anti-Semitic *pogroms* of Eastern Europe. Only a few vestiges remain of this Jewish community: the registrar of an old people's home, where the Gestapo later rounded up Jews to deport them to a concentration camp; a ritual silver candelabra for a Sabbath table; a school bulletin from a children's home; an empty silver-and-black cardboard hatbox from a local milliner.

Berlin's first Jewish Museum, inaugurated at 31 Oranienburger Strasse on January 24, 1933, a week prior to Adolf Hitler's appointment as chancellor, was another casualty of the Nazi regime. Although the museum succeeded in organizing fourteen exhibitions devoted to different Jewish artists, it closed after *Kristallnacht*. Most of the collections, seized during the span of the Third Reich, were either lost, stolen, or found their way into other museums around the world.

Thanks to private funding, the New Synagogue's exhibition features the work of a number of artists, who once exhibited in the Jewish Museum. Among the choice paintings are two striking self-portraits by the German *Secessionist* Max Liebermann (1847–1935), and an early Expressionist canvas by Jakob Steinhardt (1887–1968), *The Prophet*, which used to hang in the museum's entrance hall. In this work, painted in 1912 when Steinhardt founded the artistic group "Die Pathetiker" with Ludwig Meidner and Richard Janthur, the city is represented as an object of apoca-

THIS TWISTED *TORCHÈRE*, UNCOVERED BENEATH THE RUBBLE, REMAINS AN ELOQUENT ARTIFACT OF THE TRAGIC EVENTS THAT TOOK PLACE IN GERMANY, BOTH BEFORE AND DURING WORLD WAR II.

THIS MAX LEIBERMANN SELF-PORTRAIT ONCE HUNG IN BERLIN'S FIRST JEWISH MUSEUM, INAUGURAT-
ED AT 31 ORANIENBURGER STRASSE ON JANUARY 24, 1933,
A WEEK PRIOR TO HITLER'S APPOINTMENT AS CHANCELLOR.
ON THE WALL IS AN EARLY EXPRESSIONIST WORK BY JACOB STEINHARDT, TITLED *THE PROPHET*.

lyptic prophecy. A desperate, terrified crowd surrounds the prophet, who warns and admonishes his followers to change their ways if they wish to avert the coming catastrophe. While the painting alludes to the imminent First World War, it also foreshadows the destruction of Berlin's Jewish community, so eloquently recounted in this exhibition.

Since 1991, Berlin's Jewish community has been formally reunited, and numbers around 10,000 members, many of them from the former Soviet Union. After Germany's reunification, and following the establishment of the Centrum Judaicum,

several Jewish institutions have been established in the vicinity of the New Synagogue (including a school). Selected photographs by Michael Kerstgens reveal the daily life and celebrations of this new and growing Jewish population.

While commemorating the unique legacy and tragic history of Berlin's Jewish community, the Centrum Judaicum also celebrates its auspicious rebirth. Seeing this important and moving exhibition, one can only hope that it will serve as a catalyst for a new era of mutual respect and understanding.

Tegel Castle

Gabrielenstrasse
D-130507 Berlin
Tel: 434–3156

Open Monday
10:00 A.M. to Noon and
3:00 P.M. to 5:00 P.M.
May 1 to September 30
Visits only by guided tour, which
must be arranged in advance.

U-Bahn: 6 to Tegel
Bus: 124, 125, 133, 224, 815

MINUTES away from Tegel Airport, the enterprising visitor will discover at the end of a tree-lined dirt road one of the most harmonious and compelling edifices to be found on the outskirts of Berlin: Schloss Tegel, the former castle and property of Wilhelm von Humboldt (1767–1835), the renowned German statesman, linguist, and educator, whose progressive views and erudition have often prompted scholars to liken him to America's Thomas Jefferson.

Beautifully maintained and preserved by one of Humboldt's descendants, Ulrich von Heinz, the castle offers visitors the opportunity to admire the felicitous relationship between Prussia's greatest architect

THE REAR OF SCHLOSS TEGEL
IS CROWNED WITH AN AIRY LOGGIA AND SET OFF BY CORNER TOWERS
THAT ARE ADORNED WITH RELIEFS
REPRESENTING THE GODS OF THE WINDS INSPIRED BY
THE TOWER OF WINDS IN ATHENS.

Karl Friedrich Schinkel and its erudite owner. Originally a hunting lodge built around 1550 for the Great Elector Joachim II (1535–1571) on property overlooking hillside vineyards and the Tegeler See, the largest and most beautiful of the Havel lakes, it was acquired in 1765 by the Humboldts, a prominent family of Berlin intellectuals. Wilhelm von Humboldt, who had befriended Schinkel during his stay in Rome as Prussian ambassador in 1804–1805, commissioned the architect to transform the rustic castle into a Neoclassical edifice, which he did from 1820 to 1824. The architect devised a three-story manor house, crowning it with a loggia, and setting it off with four corner towers, adorned with reliefs representing eight gods of the winds made by the workshop of Christian Daniel Rauch and inspired by the Tower of Winds in Athens.

Although it was first used as a summer home, Schloss Tegel was to become a year-round refuge from the repressive Karlsbad Decrees, which took their toll on Prussian intellectual and academic life, and ultimately drove the broad-minded Humboldt to resign from public affairs. Despite this setback, the Prussian statesman was nonetheless able to look back on a career replete with achievements. Under his inspired leadership and administration as Prussia's Minister of Education, he founded Berlin's first university in 1810. That same year, he introduced state examinations for teachers and created a secondary school or *Gymnasium*, based on humanist values and focusing on the study of Latin, Greek, German, and mathematics. His ultimate aim was to establish a compulsory educational system that would prepare his countrymen to meet their responsibilities in a liberal state. (Despite the far-

THE MONUMENTAL ANTIQUITIES ROOM, CONSIDERED TO BE THE FIRST MUSEUM IN PRUSSIA, IS ADORNED WITH PLASTER COPIES OF FRIEZES FROM THE PARTHENON. IT ALSO BOASTS ONE OF THE MOST ADMIRED SCULPTURES OF THE PERIOD: A PLASTER CAST OF THE JUNO LUDOVISI, WHICH INSPIRED A POEM BY GOETHE.

THE HEAD ON THIS ROMAN MARBLE SYLPH IS THAT OF HUMBOLDT'S
ELDEST DAUGHTER CAROLINA, SCULPTED BY CHRISTIAN DANEL RAUCH.
THE TWO PLASTER PORTRAIT MEDALLIONS
ARE OF WILHELM AND HIS BROTHER ALEXANDER.

reaching impact of Humboldt's ideals, the Prussian government lacked both the financial resources and political attitudes to implement them. Not until the establishment of the Prussian Constitution in 1850 did education become free to all.)

A guided tour of Schloss Tegel not only shows the genteel existence that Humboldt enjoyed with his learned spouse, Carolina, and their seven children, but also reveals the family's passion for the antique. The downstairs indoor atrium, which is set off by two Doric columns, suggests the entrance to a Grecian temple. Here, pride of place is given to the most important piece in Humboldt's collection, the marble fountain of Saint Callistus from the second century A.D. (Saint Callistus was a Roman pope who extended forgiveness to many sinners whose transgressions were thought to be unforgivable.) Two casts of ancient Greek wall friezes, one representing The Three Fates, the other showing a Grecian-looking Apollo making an offering to a goddess in a more modern Roman temple, demonstrates Humboldt's concern with uniting past and present, both personally and philosophically, explains von Heinz. "While he was against the French Revolution in 1793 on the one hand, he also was quite keen on making reforms in Prussia," he notes. "Rather than working in behalf of revolutions, he worked to establish civil rights and reforms, such as his 1812 Edict of Tolerance that was extended to Prussia's Jews."

In the jade-green downstairs study, plaster casts of the Venus de Milo and the Venus Capitoline stand like sentinels guarding the desk where Humboldt kept up with his voluminous correspondence and prepared many of his papers on linguistics. His writings on language, which posited that every individual speaks his own personal language (considered to be a rather radical idea during his lifetime), were published after his death. It is only today that Humboldt's views are being taken seriously by such noted linguists as Noam Chomsky, according to von Heinz. Regrettably, Humboldt's precious library, buried for safekeeping in Mecklenburg during World War II, along with other rarities, was either lost or burned.

In the upstairs Blauer or Blue Salon, painted a vivid "Schinkel blue," and decorated with a stencil frieze painted in tempera, there is an informal arrangement of sofas, tables, and chairs that could easily be moved to accommodate a small circle of intimates—a room layout characteristic of the bourgeois sociability of the

early-nineteenth-century Biedermeier period. Among the salon's striking statuary are two plaster portrait medallions of Wilhelm and Alexander, handsomely set off by a Roman marble sylph whose head is that of

UNABLE TO AFFORD MARBLE PEDESTALS TO SUPPORT HIS ANTIQUE STATUARY, HUMBOLDT COMMISSIONED ROTATING WOODEN BASES THAT WERE PAINTED TO RESEMBLE MARBLE.

Humboldt's eldest daughter, Carolina, sculpted by Christian Daniel Rauch. (The origin of the term "Biedermeier" comes from *bieder*, a derogatory word for bourgeois, and *meier*, the German equivalent of Jones or Brown; put together, it meant cozy respectability.)

Adjacent to this charming family room is the monumental Antiquities Room, considered to be the first museum in Prussia, since it was opened five years before Schinkel's Altes Museum (Old Museum), which was built between 1825 and 1830. Working in close collaboration,

Schinkel and Rauch decorated this magnificent Neoclassical room, which still retains its star-studded ceiling decoration, albeit somewhat faded as a result of subsequent flooding and mildew. Many of the works in the room were gifts from Pope Pius VII,

THIS PORPHYRY COPY OF THE MEDUSA RONDANINI WAS GIVEN TO WILHELM VON HUMBOLT BY POPE PIUS VII, WHO WISHED TO EXPRESS HIS GRATITUDE TO THE DIPLOMAT FOR SUCCEEDING IN RESTORING MANY WORKS TAKEN BY NAPOLEON FROM THE VATICAN MUSEUM AND THE VILLA BORGHESE.

who was grateful to Humboldt for succeeding in restoring many works taken by Napoleon from the Vatican Museum and the Villa Borghese. (Ironically, Humboldt's family was to suffer similar depredations during World War II, when the Soviet Red Army took away many valuable pieces, only to return most of them in 1958 to the former German Democratic Republic. Still, it wasn't until the fall of the Berlin Wall in 1990, that these antiquities, including the priceless Saint Callistus fountain and two Roman marble torsos, were returned to Schloss Tegel.)

As a devoted Classicist, Humboldt was proud to own copies of some of the most admired sculpted works of his time: a plaster cast of the enormous head of the Juno Ludovisi (which had inspired a poem by Goethe), a porphyry copy of the Medusa Rondanini, as well as plaster copies of friezes from the Parthenon. So taken was he by the striking first century A.D. granite obelisk on the Spanish Steps in Rome, that he commissioned a small replica of it for his Antiquities Room, with two matching tables topped with the same stone. Designed by Schinkel, both the obelisk and the tables are made from granite taken from the original monument, something that would be unthinkable today.

Two small sitting rooms that open onto the opposite end of the Antiquities Room demonstrate the continuity that Humboldt strove to maintain between his own era and the ancient world. In one of these rooms is Bertel Alberto Thorwaldsen's *Goddess of Hope,* a copy of which was made for the cemetery behind Schloss Tegel, where Wilhelm and his brother Alexander, the renowned naturalist and explorer, are buried. Thorwaldsen (1770–1844) was a Danish Neoclassical sculptor who had studied in Rome and was to become the second most influential sculptor of his time, second only to Canova. He also sculpted Humboldt's twelve-year-old daughter Adelaide holding a butterfly, underscoring the young girls' transformation from puberty to womanhood.

"Humboldt wanted to have three sitting rooms that all opened onto the Antiquities Room," notes von Heinz. "This way you were always encountering ancient art, considered to be the most important art at the time. Humboldt believed that you formed your character and feelings seeing such works of art, and that is

a far less costly decorative solution compared to silk wall hangings or carved moldings. Instead of building an expensive marble or stone staircase to the second floor, the wooden staircase was painted to resemble marble.

Seeing the ways in which Schloss

THE BLUE SALON, PAINTED A BRILLIANT "SCHINKEL BLUE," FEATURES AN INFORMAL ARRANGEMENT OF SOFAS, TABLES, AND CHAIRS, CHARACTERISTIC OF THE BOURGEOIS SOCIABILITY OF THE BIEDERMEIER PERIOD.

why these antiquities are close to the everyday living quarters and not in another part of the residence."

While Humboldt and Schinkel revered the antique, they also valued low-cost aesthetic solutions to accommodate a relatively modest budget. Unable to afford marble pedestals to support his antique statuary, Humboldt commissioned rotating wooden bases instead, painted to resemble marble. The stairwell leading to the second floor is covered with gorgeous hand-painted Pompeiian-style wallpaper, probably manufactured in Schinkel's workshop,

Tegel is a unique blend of the antique and the innovative, the magnificent and the economical, one gains insight not only into Wilhelm von Humboldt's tastes and interests, but also into his character and philosophy.

"Wilhelm von Humboldt used to say that even if his books and theories vanished, Schloss Tegel would express, by its architecture and antiquities and the arrangement of its rooms, his fundamental beliefs," says von Heinz. A visit to Schloss Tegel only serves to confirm Humboldt's farsighted prediction.

The Berlin Teddy Museum

147 Kurfürstendamm
10709 Berlin
Tel: 893–39–65

Open Wednesday, Thursday, and
Friday
3:00 P.M. to 6:00 P.M.
Group visits available with advance
reservations.

Bus: 129 to Leninerplatz

THIS MUCH-LOVED TEDDY FAMILY
INCLUDES A TINY
BERLIN BEAR IN A MINIATURE
HIGH-CHAIR.

STROLLING down the bustling Kurfürstendamm, famous for its enticing shop windows filled with the finest Meissen china and the most delectable pastries and chocolates, it's hard to imagine that this celebrated avenue also contains a spacious, modern four-room apartment dedicated to the exhibition of a staggering number of adorable, fuzzy stuffed animals in every conceivable color, shape, and size. Nonetheless, passionate and knowledgeable collectors know that the discreet teddy bear illustration taped next to the apartment's outdoor buzzer indicates the Berlin Teddy Museum—which the Guinness Book of World Records claims is the "largest teddy bear museum" on the planet. With over 3,000 bears and other stuffed animals in residence, few would dare to quibble with such a claim.

It's difficult to say what is more astonishing—the size and scope of this collection, or the knowledge and commitment of its owner, Florentine C. Bredow, who has turned her childhood predilection for stuffed animals into a tireless pursuit dedicated to collecting and preserving the greatest possible number of toy bears imaginable. "My interest in bears dates from my childhood collection, which I had from the time I was five or six years old," she recalls. "My parents were antique specialists and it was natural for us to collect things." During World War II, when her family was forced to flee their estate in Braunschweig near Hanover, among the few things her parents took along were her father's teddy bears. This was to form the core of

what is considered today to be a priceless collection, with some antique bears fetching prices of 20,000 DM, if not more.

Bredow's passion for teddy bears took a more scholarly turn when she translated an American book on the history of the stuffed animal into German in the 1970s. As her home ran out of space to store all her teddies, she began actively seeking a museum in which to display them. When the Charlottenburg Palace Museum turned down her collection—much to her disappointment—she decided to open her own museum in 1986 in a handsomely furnished penthouse apartment overlooking the skyline of Berlin.

"The museum is a huge success," exults the blond and jovial Bredow, who takes great pride in showing the twelve guestbooks signed by visitors from as far away as Hong Kong and Tokyo. "I have even inherited some teddies," she notes. "It shows just how much a teddy bear means to a person. One old woman had included her teddy in her will—it was to be put in the grave with her. She then heard about my museum and after her death I inherited her teddy bear. It is now on display in the museum."

Only Bredow has the ability to locate this teddy among the thousands on display. There are bears literally everywhere: peeping out of cupboards, tucked away in closets, huddled together in floor-to-ceiling bookcases covered with chickenwire, lying on beds and sprawling on couches, poised like proud soldiers and dapper gentlemen on every available tabletop or desk. Nor is that all. A daunting array of multicolored miniature plastic, rubber, and glass bears are tidily displayed in glass cases hanging from the walls, while plush bears await their *toilette* in the plushly carpeted bathroom. Still, there is no bear that hasn't been given its proper place in this enchanting museum which appeals to the child in all of us—whether it be the oldest bears on four wheels dating from around 1900, to the "wounded" bears whose arms, ears, and eyes have been lost, after much wear and tear.

With the fall of the Berlin Wall in 1990, velour-covered "Red bears" from the former East Berlin, as well as pink, black, and yellow rubber bears from Thuringia were also added to the collection, thus demonstrating that bears in all shapes, colors, and sizes have always retained their significance in Germany, regardless of political differences.

It seems appropriate that Berlin should harbor the world's first and largest teddy bear museum, given that the bear has been a common sight in the region since the Middle Ages, and has been featured on the city's seal since 1280. (The current seal of Berlin depicts an upright crowned black bear with a thrusting red tongue and claws.)

Touring the museum, it is apparent that the toy bear has undergone quite a number of changes since it was first manufactured. Like a seasoned anthropologist, Bredow documents the evolution of the plush animal, whose shape and material has changed in a number of ways over the years. "The first toy bears had reinforced bodies and were on four wheels so children could either ride them or pull them around. When they started to make bears that were standing up, they took away their tail," recalls Bredow. "They made the teddy bear more human. Remember, when man stood up, he also lost his tail," she adds.

The shape and material of teddies has also evolved. According to Bredow, the nose has become flatter, as well as the rest of the face. Whereas the first teddies had shoe-button eyes and were made of mohair, nowadays they have plastic eyes and are made with synthetic, flame-retardant materials, which are less hazardous to children.

The classic stuffed bear was named Teddy after America's twenty-sixth President, and this was inspired by a cartoon by Clifford Berryman in a 1902 issue of the *Washington Star* showing President Theodore Roosevelt, standing rifle in hand with his back turned to a towering bear cub; the caption read "Drawing the line in Mississippi." The cartoon, which received nationwide attention, underscored Roosevelt's attempt to settle a border dispute between Louisiana and Mississippi, while showing the President's refusal to kill a trapped bear cub and bring him home as a trophy. It was this very cartoon that inspired Morris Michton, a Russian-immigrant toy salesman from Brooklyn, New York, to make a stuffed bear cub and place it alongside the cartoon in his store window. The attention-getting bear attracted customers, and it wasn't long before Michton was manufacturing stuffed bears with shoe-button eyes called Teddy's Bear.

At around the same time, German toy manufacturer Margaret Steiff also began producing stuffed bear cubs. Steiff, whose company remains a respected name in the stuffed-toy industry to this day, was a polio victim confined to a wheelchair. In the 1880s, she began sewing felt animals by hand. The German toy

A CHINA CUPBOARD OVERFLOWS
WITH HUNDREDS OF BEARS IN ALL SHAPES AND SIZES.
ONLY THE MUSEUM'S DIRECTOR
CAN ENUMERATE AND DESCRIBE THEM ALL.

inspired scores of imitations all over the world. Visitors take a special interest in comparing the appearance of bears from different countries, whether they be the British *Rupert*, *Winnie-the-Pooh*, and *Paddington* bears, the Russian *Michka*, the German *Bussi*, or the cartoon-inspired *Baloo* from Walt Disney's version of Rudyard Kipling's *The Jungle Book*. Among Bredow's favorites are such "celebrity" teddies, as Frederick the Great, Queen Elizabeth I and her sister, Mary, Queen of Scots, as well as the "Karl Lagerfeld" bear who sports the couturier's trademark silver ponytail, black-framed dark glasses, and black fan. There is even a "Christo" bear wrapped up in cotton sacking and twine, inspired by the conceptual artist who wrapped the Reichstag building in 1996.

The sentimental and therapeutic value of teddies is almost as great as the prices they command at auction. "Teddy bears are used to help children talk through traumatic experiences, and are also used in hospitals, particularly after thoracic and abdominal surgery," Bredow explains. Still, sometimes, the emotion of seeing a particular teddy bear can prove overwhelming for the visitor. "The conversations I overhear in the museum are astounding," Bredow maintains. "Visitors will see a teddy on display that reminds them of a bear from their childhood. There are times when I am afraid some people will have heart attacks, they get so excited." Judging by the enthusiastic and appreciative comments in the museum's guest-book, Bredow need not worry. The comfort and joy that comes from visiting this museum is perhaps best summed up by one visitor who wrote in a guestbook: "A teddy bear makes life bearable."

THIS TEDDY BEAR STRUTS ITS STUFF IN A BELLY-DANCER OUTFIT.

manufacturer claims that, shortly after the Clifford Berryman cartoon was published, an American visitor to the Steiff factory showed Margaret Steiff the illustration, and suggested that she make a plush toy bear with its likeness. When Steiff's bears made their debut at the 1904 Leipzig Fair, the company was besieged with orders.

So great was the success of the Michton and Steiff bears that, throughout this century, they have

THIS UNIQUE "TEDDY WALL HANGING,"
WHICH DOMINATES THE LIVING ROOM, HAS BEEN SHOWN
IN TEDDY BEAR EXHIBITS ALL OVER GERMANY.

Museum of Prehistory and Early History

**Schloss Charlottenburg
Langhansbau
14059 Berlin
Tel: 32091–233**

**Open Tuesday through Friday
10:00 A.M. to 6:00 P.M.;
Saturday and Sunday
11:00 A.M. to 6:00 P.M.**

**U-Bahn: 7 to Richard Wagner
Platz
Bus: 109, 110, 145, X21, X26**

THE PREHISTORY AND EARLY HISTORY
MUSEUM IS LOCATED IN THE NEOCLASSICAL
FORMER THEATER BUILDING IN THE
CHARLOTTENBURG CASTLE.

HEINRICH Schliemann's (1822–1890) tireless determination to excavate ancient Troy had its beginnings at the age of seven, when his father, a young impoverished pastor from Mecklenburg, showed him an illustration of Homeric Troy in the *Universal History for Children.* Knowing the miserable circumstances of Schliemann's childhood, and the long, hard years of penury that followed, it is not only remarkable that he never lost sight of his dream, but that he was able to create the conditions necessary to fulfill it. Then again, Schliemann was no ordinary man. Even while working as a commercial clerk in Amsterdam, he managed to learn a number of languages rather rapidly, mastering them in a matter of weeks. Because of his exceptional linguistic proficiency, his Dutch employer sent him to Saint

THIS DISPLAY OF HEINRICH SCHLIEMANN'S FINDS
FROM TROY INCLUDES MANY HANDSOME PIECES OF CERAMIC POTTERY.
(PHOTO: STAATLICHE MUSEEN ZU BERLIN-PREUSSISCHER
KULTURBESITZ MUSEUM FÜR VOR- UND FRÜHGESCHICHTE)

Petersburg, Russia, where he amassed a fortune during the Crimean War, selling indigo, weapons, and armaments.

Yet, even after becoming an independently wealthy man, Schliemann never lost sight of his goal. After retiring from business in 1863, he traveled around the world, then began studying archaeology in Paris in 1866, and completed his doctorate at the University of Rostock three years later. His thesis was based on the results of his travels and investigations of the Mycenaean world, in Greece and Asia Minor. In 1870 he began investigating the large *tell* of Hissarlik, which he took to be Homeric Troy. His unprecedented dig was to uncover seven overlapping layers and reach a depth of seventeen meters. Soon afterward, he published a treatise asserting that he had indeed discovered the site of the Trojan War, a claim that initially incited derision from leading scholars in the field.

(At that time, two rival schools existed, one contending that Homer's *Iliad* and *Odyssey* were based on a collection of folktales related over the centuries by minstrels, while others thought these epics arose from the imagination of a poetic genius.)

Schliemann, of course, thought otherwise, following the Greek poet's writings slavishly, so that he assigned all his finds to the Homeric heroes—which was a mistake. It is well known today that the famed "Priam's Treasure" of gold jewelry and ceremonial axes that he unearthed did not come from the Homeric level at Hissarlik, but dated back a thousand years before the fall of Troy (c. 1250 B.C.). Moreover, the Shaft Graves discovered at Mycenae were not the burial places of Agamemnon and his family, as Schliemann believed, but belonged to an earlier phase of the Bronze Age.

On the other hand, Schliemann did discover Troy, did prove the

Homeric epics were based on history, and did reveal the Bronze Age background in Homer's work. His greatest find was the famous Shaft graves, which despite earlier depredations, still contained their princely owners lying with their splendid vessels of gold and silver, their exquisitely ornamented weapons and their gold death masks, which are now exhibited in Athens' Archaeological Museum.

(When it came to "Priam's Treasure" Schliemann was reluctant to part with his finds. Although initially the archaeologist promised to put back the pieces he had exhumed, he ended up paying the rulers of the declining Ottoman Empire 50,000 francs in gold, a sum that he estimated gave him sole proprietorship over this priceless haul.)

Today, visitors to the Museum of Prehistory and Early History, can learn more about Schliemann and his excavations at Troy. (In 1881, Schliemann, avid for official recognition, donated 10,000 artifacts, including "Priam's Treasure" to the German people.)

Among the discoveries presented in the handsomely mounted exhibition are polished marble, owl-like talismans (possibly related to the cult of Athena, whose mascot was the owl, the symbol of wisdom), clay spinning wheels, terra-cotta pottery, as well as large clay storage vessels with pointed bases, once used for storing oil, wine, and grain. Sadly absent, however, is the legendary "Priam's Treasure"— long thought to have been destroyed during the last war. In 1991, the magazine *ARTnews* revealed that this stupendous hoard, which had been kept in three crates since 1941 in a virtually impregnable flak tower near the Berlin Zoo, had been removed from Germany by the Soviet Army at the end of World War II. After a hiatus of more than fifty years, on October 24, 1994, staff members from the Museum of Prehistory and Early History were permitted to inspect the Schliemann treasures that had been languishing for decades in the basement of the Pushkin Museum in Moscow and the Hermitage Museum in Saint Petersburg.

"It's kind of an ironic twist of fate, knowing that Schliemann first offered his Trojan treasures to the Russian Tsar," notes senior curator Dr. Klaus Goldmann. "However, the Tsar refused his gift, maintaining that it was impossible for him to accept it from a man who had divorced a Russian woman. Schliemann divorced his first wife in the United States, because she did not share his passion for archaeology. It took the Red Army to get their hands on this treasure," he adds, with a chuckle.

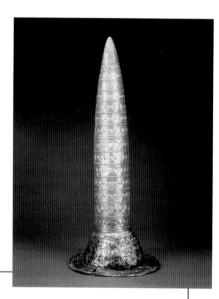

THIS UNUSUAL BRONZE AGE GOLD HAT, DISCOVERED IN SOUTHERN GERMANY, MAY HAVE BEEN WORN DURING PRIESTLY RITUALS. (PHOTO: STAATLICHE MUSEEN ZU BERLIN-PREUSSISCHER KULTURBESITZ MUSEUM FÜR VOR-UND FRÜHGESCHICHTE).

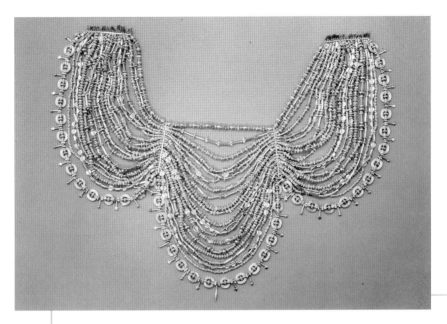

THIS GOLD-PLATED NECKLACE, INSPIRED BY THE STRINGS OF GOLD BEADS
SCHLIEMANN UNCOVERED AT TROY,
WAS MADE BY THE MASTER GOLDSMITH WOLFGANG KUCKENBERG.
THE ORIGINAL GOLD BEADS WERE TAKEN BY THE RED ARMY IN 1945
AND ARE NOW EXHIBITED IN MOSCOW'S PUSHKIN MUSEUM.
(PHOTO: STAATLICHE MUSEEN ZU BERLIN-PREUSSISCHER KULTURBESITZ
MUSEUM FÜR VOR- UND FRÜHGESCHICHTE).

Despite its comparatively small size, visitors are bound to be impressed by the diversity of this exceptional museum, whose origins stem from the collections of art and antiquities of the Hohenzollerns. Divided into four departments, its finds range from the Old and Middle Stone Ages (going as far back as 50,000 years ago), the Neolithic Period (6000–3000 B.C.), the Bronze Age (3000–800 B.C.), to the early Medieval period (c. A.D. 1100). The ground floor traces the development of man and the earliest cultures, documenting the life of cave dwellers from the Paleolithic era to the end of the Ice Age, followed by the spread of agriculture and livestock raising to the invention of ceramics and the establishment of the first cities in the Near East.

The biggest eye-opener is in the second-floor exhibition area, devoted to illustrating the comparatively sophisticated civilization of the Bronze Age, a period that saw the widespread adoption of bronze metallurgy across Europe. For a long time, it was supposed that the Mediterreanean was not only the cradle of civilization, but that its trade connections established by the Minoan and Mycenaean civilizations based in the southern part of mainland Greece had important cultural consequences for the rest of Europe. Now, thanks to radiocarbon dating, it has been established that highly evolved Bronze Age cultures existed in parts of Northern Europe, including Germany, several centuries *before* these Mediterranean civilizations reached their peak, a premise which is extensively illustrated and documented in this museum.

Intricately detailed dioramas help visitors to imagine Europe's early Bronze Age settlements, as well as the continent's first copper and tin mines, dating back to 3000 B.C., which were located in Austria's Alpine region, in Germany's Harz Mountains, as well as in Bohemia. By 2000 B.C., most of Europe had adopted copper-tin alloys for making bronze, thus creating bronze-dependent societies. "The Iron Age followed the Bronze Age because the ores needed to make iron were harder to get at, and the making of iron required more fuel than bronze," explains Dr. Goldmann. "At that time, iron was worth more than gold."

A remarkable and little-known aspect of the Bronze Age is that regions in northern and central Europe, although lacking in metal ores, were nonetheless able to successfully establish metal-working traditions. Their demand for metal laid the basis for an enduring trade network among different regions, and created a new entrepreneurial class that controlled the metal's production and distribution. The development and elaboration of metallurgy spurred a range of new fabrication possibilities and designs for bronze weapons, shields, agricultural tools, jewelry, and cult objects. For instance, the museum's Bronze Age helmets and armor (which were discovered in Slovenia in 1903), reveal that Etruscan metalworkers plied their trade throughout Central and Northern Europe.

While the museum boasts an

THIS MODERN PORTRAIT BUST OF HOMER, EXECUTED IN 1875
BY THE NEOPOLITAN SCULPTOR GAETANO ROSSI,
OVERLOOKS THE *KOLASSOL PITHORI*,
LARGE STORAGE VESSELS THAT WERE ONCE USED FOR STORING WINE, OIL,
GRAIN, AND OTHER FOODSTUFFS.
THEY WERE FOUND IN ANCIENT STOREROOMS AT TROY WITH THEIR POINTED
BASES DUG INTO THE GROUND. (PHOTO: STAATLICHE MUSEEN ZU BERLIN-PREUSSISCHER
KULTURBESITZ MUSEUM FÜR VOR- UND FRÜHGESCHICHTE)

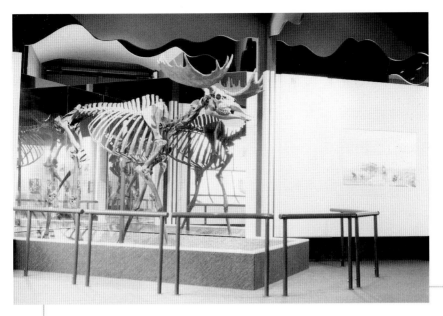

THE SKELETON OF THIS PREHISTORIC REINDEER WAS UNCOVERED IN BERLIN
AFTER WORLD WAS II WHEN THE CITY'S U-BAHN WAS BEING BUILT.
(PHOTO: STAATLICHE MUSEEN ZU BERLIN-PREUSSISCHER KULTURBESITZ MUSEUM
FÜR VOR- UND FRÜHGESCHICHTE)

extensive collection of ancient weapons, implements, and jewelry found in Bronze Age tombs during the construction of Berlin's Autobahn, its most valuable Bronze Age find has been missing since the war—the Gold Treasure of Eberswalde, a collection of gold jewelry, cups, and implements, named after the town in Brandenburg where it was unearthed. It has been widely documented that this priceless discovery—the largest ever made in Germany—was taken by the Soviet Red Army from the same flak tower and the same crate where the Schliemann hoard was hidden.

During the European Migration period—from the fourth to the seventh centuries A.D.—coinciding with the decline of the Roman Empire and culminating with the consolidation of the Frankish peoples under the rule of the Merovingians—there existed an extensive and complex Germanic civi-lization that left a lasting mark on both Europe and Africa, as demon-strated by the museum's extensive displays of elegant ceramics, metal-work, and stone statuary. "Long before Berlin was founded in the thir-teenth century, a prosperous and complex culture had developed here," notes Dr. Goldmann. "Often the only way to uncover it is through archaeo-logical digs, because there are so few written texts. The foreign goods, cus-toms seals, coins, and jewelry that have been found, help us to achieve an understanding of the economy and evolution of medieval man," he notes.

Visitors who spend time in this compelling, thought-provoking museum are bound to gain exciting new insights into the importance of archaeology, not only in the unearth-ing of ancient treasures, but also in providing a more accurate vision of the past.

THIS NEOCLASSICAL SILVER SUGAR BOWL
WITH VERMEIL SPOONS
SHOWS THAT WHEN SUGAR
WAS FIRST USED
IT WAS CONSIDERED A PRECIOUS LUXURY,
RATHER THAN A HOUSEHOLD STAPLE.

Sugar Museum

Amrumer Strasse 32
13353 Berlin (Wedding)
Tel: 31–42–75–74

Open Monday through Wednesday
9:00 A.M. to 5:00 P.M.
Sunday 11:00 A.M. to 6:00 P.M.

U-Bahn: 9 to Amrumer Strasse or
6 to Seestrasse
Bus: 126, 328

Sometimes a significant invention will be condemned to oblivion until economic and political circumstances favor its implementation. Such has been the case with beet sugar, first discovered in Berlin in 1747 by the noted Prussian chemist Andreas Sigismund Marggraf (1709–1782). Almost another half-century would lapse before his student and successor, Franz Carl Achard (1753–1821) produced the world's first edible beet sugar. Eventually, Achard was successful in persuading Friedrich Wilhelm III that, with an investment of 50,000 thalers, Prussia could save up to *four million thalers* producing its own sugar from beets, instead of importing costly cane sugar from the colonies. Thus, in 1801, Achard opened the world's first beet sugar factory under the monarch's patronage in Cunern, Silesia (now part of Poland).

His timing could not have been better. In 1806, after occupying Prussia, Napoleon Bonaparte issued his notorious edict—the Continental Blockade—which virtually cut off British exports of cane sugar from the West Indies and Southeast Asia. After Achard's beet sugar factory opened in Silesia, Napoleon was soon urging that similar enterprises be opened elsewhere in Germany as well

THE SUGAR MUSEUM, WITH ITS PATINA-COVERED TOWER
IN THE SHAPE OF A WORLD WAR I GERMAN ARMY HELMET,
IS THE OLDEST MUSEUM OF ITS KIND IN THE WORLD.
ITS SANDSTONE PORTAL IS SURMOUNTED BY A RELIEF OF ATHENA,
THE GODDESS OF SCIENCE, AND A CORNUCOPIA OF SUGAR BEETS
BESIEGED BY LURKING MICE.

as in France and in the Netherlands. Yet, not even the enterprising Napoleon realized the potential of this new industry, which now accounts for forty percent of the world's sugar consumption.

This intriguing development in sugar production is handsomely documented in the encyclopedic Sugar Museum, which first opened in 1904 at the instigation of Edmund Oskar von Lippmann (1857–1940), Germany's first leading authority on the history and science of sugar and sugar manufacturing. This institution is the oldest of its kind in the world, featuring an extensive collection of objects in eleven thematic sections ranging from the origins of sugar, the history of cane sugar plantations and the slave trade, to beet cultivation, beet sugar production, and derivative products made from sugar.

Visiting this museum one comes to realize the staggering number of products that contain sugar or its derivatives, including all wines and champagnes, most alcoholic beverages and beer (German beer being a notable exception), all sorts of processed foods, as well as animal feed, medicine, plant food, and even shampoo. Since the sixteenth century, sugar has also been used to produce intricate spun-sugar sculptures—an art form perfected in Italy—and this far-ranging collection boasts some outstanding examples, including a replica of the famed Teahouse at Sanssouci and of Berlin's Brandenburg Gate.

However, one of the exhibits shows that human ingenuity can also produce lethal consequences: the museum's most shocking item is a container of Zyklon-B, the poison gas used in concentration camps, which was made from crushed leaves taken from the sugar beet.

It is surprising to learn the extent

THIS MODEL OF A 1920S BEET SUGAR FACTORY IN GERMANY
CLOSELY RESEMBLES THE PLANTS THAT WERE BUILT IN THE FORMER EAST GERMANY.

PRIMITIVE SUGAR REFINING EQUIPMENT
CONSISTED OF A CLAY FUNNEL AND POT, SUCH AS THOSE SHOWN HERE,
WHICH DEPENDED ON EXTRACTING SUGAR WATER FROM THE CANE;
THE EVAPORATION PROCESS COULD TAKE UP TO
SIX MONTHS BEFORE THE PRIZED SUGAR CRYSTALS COULD BE OBTAINED.

to which this single commodity has been used to illustrate commemorative coins, bank notes, stamps, and caricatures. It has even inspired 125 songs from all over the world, which are in the museum's extensive archives.

The exhibition reveals that, at first, the human sweet tooth had to content itself with honey, as well as date and palm sugar. Both Egyptian and Roman confectioners relied on honey, as well as herbs, spices, nuts, and fruit juices to flavor their candies. In the seventeenth century, American colonists used maple sugar taken from maple trees as a substitute for costly imported cane sugar.

It is supposed that cane sugar originated in the South Pacific around 8000 B.C. A collection of watercolors of different cane sugar varieties painted during an 1867 expedition to New Caledonia is a visual testimonial to this island's importance as the country where cane sugar was first grown. Not until 4000 B.C. did sugar become known in the West, through one of Alexander the Great's Greek generals, who—upon returning from a campaign in India—recounted that he had seen a "miraculous reed," able to produce a honey-like substance without the intervention of bees.

Sugarcane handling and the methods for making sugar spread from India to Indochina, and westward to Arabia until it finally reached Europe in the thirteenth and fourteenth centuries. The Venetians, among Europe's most sophisticated traders, developed the first large-scale sugar import trade, and the first significant candy manufacturing on the Continent.

Visitors can see the oldest type of sugar-refining equipment in the world, consisting of a clay funnel and pot (c. A.D. 1450), which depended on extracting sugar water from the cane, then an evaporation process of between three to six months, before the prized white sugar crystals could be obtained. Among the museum's other unusual exhibits are a massive sixteenth-century Chinese two-wheel stone mill; an iron "Kolu" with vertical press wheels still in use on small village farms in India; a tiger-wood sugarcane press from Colombia, South America, as well as an extraordinarily detailed, lifelike scale-model of the first sugar-beet processing factory opened by Achard.

The discovery of beet sugar also helped end one of the grisliest chapters in history: the enslavement of Africans which, for over 350 years, provided workers for most of the backbreaking labor in the cane-sugar plantations and mills in the New World, first in the Caribbean, then in Brazil. Displays of shackles and leg irons, models of Spanish, Dutch, French, and German slavers, as well as documents, engravings, and photos, demonstrate the different facets of this barbaric trade, which was to uproot and destroy millions of lives.

As early as 1506, Spain had begun cultivating sugar in the Greater Antilles, on the string of islands dominated by Cuba and Hispaniola. Faced with a decline in the native population and a labor shortage, it resorted to importing slaves from Africa to work its plantations and sugar mills. In 1515, Spain sent its first consignment of slaves directly from Africa to America, and received its first shipment of slave-grown and harvested American sugar. After Spain began to exploit the New World's gold and silver, it fell to the Portuguese to discover the profit

that could be made from combining slaving in Africa with sugar production in Brazil. Backed by the authority of Pope Nicholas V, they were told to "attack, subject, and reduce to perpetual slavery the Saracens, pagans, and other enemies of Christ southward from Capes Badjor and Non, including all the coast of Guinea." The monarchs and merchants from West Africa's Gold Coast were more than willing to oblige, exchanging unwanted people for cloth, firearms, iron hardware, and alcohol. Occasionally, there was a murmur of protest, but it was too muted to compete with the demands of the Brazilian sugar producers to work, as one planter wrote, "half a year together night and day like horses." In 1550 there were five sugar plantations in Brazil; by 1623, there were three hundred and fifty.

It was at this stage that the Dutch became involved, invading and occupying the entire northern part of Brazil and wresting the Gold Coast from Portugal. Although they only held the Brazilian market for nineteen years, they learned a good deal about sugar production and their knowledge soon filtered through to the English, French, and Danes, who had independently acquired several Caribbean islands. The demand for slaves skyrocketed: it is estimated that during the sixteenth century fewer than one million Africans were landed in the Americas; by the eighteenth century it was seven times that number. By the time the slave trade had ended, some fifteen million Africans had been seized and shipped to the Western Hemisphere; of those, perhaps only eleven or twelve million landed alive.

In the meantime, because the Reformation's campaign against monasteries had resulted in a substantial decline in the supply of honey

THIS ARCHITECTURAL MODEL
OF THE CHINESE TEAHOUSE
AT SANSSOUCI IN POTSDAM IS MADE OF
HARD SUGAR CANDY.

THIS DEEP BLUE GLASS
AND SILVER-ORNAMENTED SUGAR BOWL
IS DECORATED WITH
VINES AND MEDALLIONS.

(the need for beeswax candles had once made these monasteries Europe's top honey producers), cane sugar usage became more widespread. By the 1670s, sugar was a trading commodity of such importance that the Dutch yielded New York to England in exchange for the sugar plantations of Suriname, while in 1763, France abandoned the whole of Canada to the British for the sake of the sugarcane production on Guadeloupe.

Over time, European farmers were able to increase the sugar content in beets through successful experimentation in selecting and growing genetically superior plants, and industrialists were able to reduce the cost of sugar manufacturing. By the 1890s, Germany had become the world's number one exporter of beet sugar. A century later, it still remains a leader, with its forty-seven factories producing almost half the world's beet sugar (four million tons in 1993 alone).

Thanks to its comprehensive and creative presentation, the Sugar Museum does far more than provide visitors with an appreciation of the technological developments connected with this single substance. In offering an enlightening overview of the social struggles and transformations that sugar production has engendered, one is also able to gain a greater insight into the sweet benefits and bitter aspects of agriculture, economics, and human ingenuity.

BIBLIOGRAPHY

———◆———

Adam, Peter.
Art of the Third Reich
New York: Harry N. Abrams, Inc.,
1992.

Baer, Winfried and Ilse (Editors).
Charlottenburg Palace, Berlin
(Museen, Schlösser und Denkmäler
in Deutschland)
Belgium: Fonds Mercator Paribas,
1995.

Baer, Winfried.
Berlin Porcelain.
Washington, D.C. : Smithsonian
Institution Press, 1980.

Bergdoll, Barry.
Karl Friedrich Schinkel: An
Architecture for Prussia
New York: Rizzoli International
Publications, Inc., 1994.

Börsch-Supan, Helmut
(Translated by Mary Carroll).
The Pfaueninsel
Berlin: Brüder Hartmann GmbH
& Co., 1987.

Börsch-Supan, Helmut
(Translated by Lucinda Rennison).
Hunting Lodge Grunewald
Berlin: Felgentreff & Goebel KG,
1988.

Bröhan, Karl H.; Braig,
Rosewith; Högermann, Dieter.
Bröhan Museum Berlin
Braunschweig: Georg Westermann
Verlag, 1996.

Craig, Norman.
Germany 1866–1945
Oxford University Press, 1981

Croucher, Penny.
Berlin: An English Guide to Known
and Unknown Treasures.
Berlin: Haude & Spener, 1987

D'Alton, Martina (Project Editor).
Along the Royal Road: Berlin
and Potsdam in KPM Porcelain and
Painting, 1815–1848
New York: The Bard Graduate Center
for Studies in the Decorative Arts, 1993.

Davies, Norman.
Europe: A History
London: Random House UK, 1997

Droysen-Reber, Dr. Dagmar; Elste,
Dr. Martin; Fellinger, Dr. Imogen;
Haase, Dr. Gesine; Wagner,
Dr. Guenther.
Museum of Musical Instruments Berlin.
Braunschweig: Georg Westermann
Verlag GmbH, 1986.

Dube, Wolf-Dieter.
The Expressionists.
London: Thames and Hudson Ltd.,
1996.

Fait, Joachim. (Translated by
John William Gabriel, with Holly
Richardson-Streese and Wendy
Wegener).
Prestel Guide Berlin
Munich: Prestel, 1992

Fuegi, John.
The Life and Lies of Bertholt Brecht
London: Flamingo, An Imprint
of HarperCollins Publishers, 1995.

Gill, Anton.
A Dance Between Flames: Berlin
Between the Wars.
London: Abacus, a division of Little,
Brown and Company, 1995.

**Goldmann, Dr. Klaus;
Strommenger, Ernst.**
Museum für Vor- und Frühgeschicte
Berlin: Staatliche Museen zu Berlin,
1995.

**Hagemann, Isolde and Zepernick,
Bernhard.**
The Berlin-Dahlem Botanic Garden
Berlin: Botanic Garden and Botanical
Museum Berlin-Dahlem, 1993

Hawkes, Jacquetta (Editor).
The World of the Past
New York: Alfred A. Knopf, Inc.,
1963.

Joestel, Dr. Volkmar.
Lutherstadt Wittenberg
Wittenberg: Drei Kastanien Verlag,
1995.

Klein, Mina C. and Klein, H. Arthur.
Käthe Kollwitz: Life in Art
New York: Schocken Books, 1975.

McLachlan, Gordon.
Berlin
Chicago: Passport Books, a division
of NTC Publishing Group, 1995

Mitford, Nancy.
Frederick the Great.
London: Penguin Books, 1995.

Moeller, Magdalena M.
"Brücke"
Munich: Hirmer Verlag GmbH,
1997.

Pakula, Hannah.
An Uncommon Woman.
New York: Simon & Schuster, 1995.

Platow, Jürgen.
Bader, Barbiere, Friseure
Berlin: FriseurMuseum, 1992

Read, Anthony and Fisher, David.
Berlin: The Biography of a City
London: Pimlico, Random House
UK, 1994.

Richard, Lionel (Editor).
Berlin, 1919–1933
*Gigantisme, crise sociale et avant-garde:
l'incarnation extrême de la modernité*
Paris: les Editions Autrement, 1993.

Schaer, Roland.
L'invention des musées
Paris: Découvertes Gallimard/Réunion
des Musées Nationaux, 1993.

**Schnell, Dr. Hugo and Steiner,
Dr. Johannes (Series Editors).**
Lutherhalle Wittenberg (English Edition)
Regensburg: Verlag Schnell & Steiner
GmbH, 1997.

Snodin, Michael (Editor).
*Karl Friedrich Schinkel: A Universal
Man*
New Haven and London: Yale
University Press,
in association with The Victoria and
Albert Museum, 1991.

Whitford, Frank.
Bauhaus.
London: Thames and Hudson, 1995.

Wingler, Hans M.
*Bauhaus-Archives Berlin (English
Edition)*
Braunschweig: Georg Westermann
Verlag, 1983.

INDEX

◆

Italic page numbers refer to illustrations. Because illustrations of façades, grounds, interiors, and holdings of featured museums are always located in the section devoted to the museum, museum main entries do not list illustration pages separately. Only *illustrated* works are listed by title.